D1250904

THE CONNERS OF CONNER PRAIRIE

THE CONNERS OF CONNER PRAIRIE

by Janet Hale

Illustrated by
Richard Day, Vincennes University

Published by
Guild Press of Indiana
and
Conner Prairie Press

PRESS

Conner Prairie Press
13400 Allisonville Road
Noblesville, IN 46060
(317) 776-6000

Guild Press of Indiana
6000 Sunset Lane
Indianapolis, IN 46208
(317) 253-0685

Library of Congress Catalog Card Number 89-080212
ISBN: 0-9617367-5-5
Hard cover trade edition

Printed in the United States
First trade edition, March 1989

TABLE OF CONTENTS

Chapter One
The Moravian Missions *1*

Chapter Two
Captured by Warring Indians in Ohio *13*

Chapter Three
White Indians in Michigan *20*

Chapter Four
White Indians in Indiana *32*

Chapter Five
Conner Store and Trading Post *45*

Chapter Six
Troubles with Tecumseh *59*

Chapter Seven
The Great Migration *72*

Chapter Eight
Horseshoe Prairie *81*

Chapter Nine
Early Indianapolis *98*

Chapter Ten
The New Town of Noblesville *111*

Conner Prairie Today *119*

Lake Michigan

Michi

Fort Wayne

Tippecanoe River

Prophetstown

Buckongahelas' Town

Anderson's Town
Horseshoe Prairie

Conner Trail

W. Conner's

Fall Creek

Indianapolis

Connersville

Fort Harrison

J. Conner's
Cedar Grove

[Indiana]

West Fork White River

Vincennes

Wabash River

Corydon.

Ohio River

New Gnadenhutten. Thames.

Detroit.

gan]

Lake Erie

Maumee River

.Lower Sandusky

Captives' Town.

.St.Mary's

White Woman's Creek

New Schoen- brunn

Schoenbrunn
.Gnadenhutten
Salem

Muskigum River

[Ohio]

Ohio River

ESSAY

OF A

Delaware-Indian and English

SPELLING-BOOK,

FOR THE

USE OF THE SCHOOLS

OF THE

CHRISTIAN INDIANS

on Muskingum River.

BY DAVID ZEISBERGER,

Missionary among the Western Indians.

Chapter One

The Moravian Missions in Ohio

It seemed as if today's school lesson would never end!
John Conner was a bright student for a six-year-old, but his
eyes kept wandering to the school's small window. Its deerskin covering was rolled up to let the late March breezes and
sunshine in.

1

The year was 1781. John's teacher was reading from a Del-a-ware Indian spelling book, and Delaware children sat beside John on the slab benches in this unusual classroom.

John's teacher was Brother David Zeisberger. He was a Moravian missionary who had come to the woods of eastern Ohio to teach the Indians the Christian religion.

Young John Conner was not thinking about either spelling or religion. "Somewhere over the hill they are making maple sugar at the sugaring camp," John thought. He looked out the window, past fields being readied for spring planting, to the woods beyond.

John could almost taste the syrup. He decided he might even let his little brother William come along after school to the sugar camp if he stayed out of the way. "Brother David will want us to work in the fields first, though," John told himself.

John drummed his fingers on the slate writing board in his lap. He was thinking about the sugar camp in the woods, where his Delaware friends laughed and joked by the steaming pots, while they waited for the syrup to boil down into candy. Soon he would be there!

After a while John felt a jab in the ribs. His Indian friend Noah, sitting next to him on the bench, was pointing at the teacher. John looked up to see Brother David gazing at him. "Can you join us for the closing hymn, John?" he said, with a smile.

All the other children had their hymn books open, and they stood and sang a hymn. The sound of children's high, sweet voices singing the old song in Lenape (Delaware) Indian language floated out the window of the school, which stood among oak trees two hundred years old.

"And now, my young brethren," said Brother David, collecting the hymn books, "we must go clear the fields for planting."

The group of Delaware Indians, and the white child filing out of the log schoolhouse were not the usual school group in

2

colonial America. And John Conner was no ordinary boy. He was a white boy completely surrounded by tribal peoples at a time when most white men were fighting for their lives against them.

He and his family lived in one of the most dangerous places in America—Ohio Country during the last years of the Revolutionary War. Yet John felt safe here in New Schoenbrunn. Here the Moravian missionaries preached that men should not fight with each other. All around the mission were other Indian tribes fighting on the British side in the Revolution, against the Americans. But inside the rule was "Do not get involved in war. It is not Christian."

The students from the school and Brother David walked to the fields behind the log cabins. There they pulled up dried cornstalks and old bean vines and took them to a pile at the edge of one of the fields. John Conner's eyes strayed to the wisp of smoke rising from the wood fire at the sugar camp in the nearby forest. Perhaps Brother David would let them go soon.

"Yes, now that it is spring, New Schoenbrunn will plant corn and vegetables, hoping the Lord will bless the harvest," Brother David was saying, as he bent over to stack the stalks for cattle fodder. John noticed that Brother David's hands were calloused from working in the fields with his "brown brethren," as he and the other missionaries called the Indians. He was a good man, John thought. And this was a good life he and his family had with these missionaries and Delawares, a life his parents had chosen because they had both been happy living with Indians themselves.

John Conner's mother, Margaret (Peggy) Boyer Conner had come to like tribal ways after she had been captured by the Shawnees when she was only six, living in Pennsylvania. During a time of trouble among Indians and settlers, Shawnees had scalped Margaret's father. Then they took Margaret and her sister to Ohio.

3

They treated the little girls well, as Indians often did children who were prisoners. They taught them the Shawnee language. Soon the girls almost forgot they were white, and they grew to like the outdoor life among the woodlands and streams of Ohio. Margaret's sister married a chief of the Shawnees.

After Margaret grew up, she fell in love with Richard Conner, a fur trader in Ohio Country who had come to trade at the Shawnee villages. When Margaret and Richard were married, both decided they liked Indian ways and wished to stay in Ohio Country. What would be the best way to do it in these days of many Indian wars? They did not know.

Then one night a man came to the door of their cabin in the wild woods. The young couple welcomed Brother Zeisberger in, and he told them he was a Moravian missionary from Bethlehem, Pennsylvania. He had come to the Ohio wilderness to build a mission for Delawares and Shawnees, where they could come and learn the Christian religion.

Margaret Conner listened all evening to Zeisberger's talk of salvation and his lovely new mission—Schoenbrunn. Richard also was interested.

"Please let us come. We want to join your Christian congregation, and we choose to live among Indians. I have been so happy for so many years among them I do not know how to live anywhere else. Schoenbrunn sounds just right for us," Margaret begged. But Brother Zeisberger would not promise.

Time passed and the Conners travelled to Pittsburgh and back. They found they did not like white cities and still wanted to live at Schoenbrunn. Finally Brother Zeisberger asked the Indians in Schoenbrunn and a Delaware chief, White Eyes, for permission for the Conners to join the mission. These Delawares agreed, and the Conner family went to join the missionaries.

4

After a while, Schoenbrunn was destroyed and a new village, New Schoenbrunn was built. Now, in 1781, Richard Conner, his wife, and their four little boys, James, John, William and baby Henry had a life as whites among Indians at New Schoenbrunn.

How would it be, John thought today as he worked in the fields side by side with Delawares, to live in a place without Indian friends? What would it be like to live the life of a white boy in a place like Philadelphia or New York? These were cities his father had told him about. John had never known anything but venison and beans, deerskin leggings and breechclout. His brothers James and little William didn't think about cities. They thought of themselves as Indians, but John didn't. He wondered about the life his father sometimes described.

Really, he did enjoy the life here at the mission. He loved to hunt, fish and canoe whenever he wished. John liked his Delaware friends, especially Noah, who was raking the fields here by his side with a wooden rake.

John especially liked sugaring with these Christian Delawares in the spring. The voice of Brother Zeisberger interrupted his thought. "The sunset hour will be coming soon, and our field work is done, young brothers," he said.

"I'll meet you at the sugar camp, Noah," John shouted in Delaware to his friend. In less than a minute John was on his way up the road to the Conner cabin.

The trail through the mission village was muddy from spring snow melt. As he hurried along, John passed small log cabins, each with its own just-spaded garden, surrounded by a picket fence. His Delaware friend Noah and Noah's mother Rebecca lived in one of these log houses.

"I'm home, Ma," John said as he walked into the Conner cabin. His little brother William came out from behind a bench where he was playing. He tugged at John's fringed, linen hunting shirt.

"Can we go sugarin' now? Can we?" William asked.

5

"I need you to go to the spring and fetch water," Margaret Conner told John. She spoke Shawnee mixed with a few English words, but he always understood her.

"Yes, Ma," John answered, but he still pulled down the sugaring sled off its peg on the log wall. "Here, William, get the sled ready. I'll be back in a while."

"Always somethin' needs doin' round here," John thought to himself. "Can't I just be on my way?" He went down the hill with a small bucket, and dipping it into a deep pool at the spring he brought up a pail of fresh, cool water.

After he had given the water to his mother, John helped William put the rude, wooden sugaring buckets on the sled. The two boys pulled the sled down the rutted path to the patches of snow at the edge of the woods. The buckets rattled around as they went over bumps on the trail to the woods.

Indians from the mission pushed past the two brothers on the trail. They were also hurrying to the sugar camp.

"Noah isn't here. He must have gone ahead of us," John told William.

Huffing and puffing, the two boys made it to the hillside grove where the maple trees had been tapped. Beyond this, down the hill, they could catch glimpses of the fire under the pots of boiling sap and smell the tangy, rich odor of boiling syrup.

"It certainly is taking a lot of work to get candy today," John said to William. "Now we need to take some of the full sap troughs off the tree to carry to the sugar pot." Everyone was expected to work for the good of the village at Schoenbrunn, and even children like John and William had to do their parts.

The boys pulled the sled over to one of the trees. A big slash had been cut two feet above the ground in this "stone tree," as the Indians called hardwood maple trees.

Slim bark funnels were sticking out of the slash, dripping sap into a fat trough made from a hollowed-out log.

6

"Well, would you look at that!" a surprised John said. "The whole trough is full, and this so near the end of the season!"

"How shall we empty the trough? It's heavy," William wondered.

"Well, you hold the bucket and I'll tip the end of the trough up. Try to hold 'er steady," John told him. So the two boys carefully tipped up the trough and emptied it a little at a time into two buckets. Then they loaded the wooden buckets onto the sled. Hurrying, they went about to two other trees, and soon the sled was heavy with buckets of maple sap.

"Let's get goin' to the boiling pots, so Rebecca can add these to the syrup," John said. He pushed the sled. William pulled with a small rope made of hemp. "Careful!" John shouted. "You're goin' too fast and it's slopping out."

"Don't order me about so, John," William said. "Just 'cause I'm younger'n you don't give you the right to boss me. Ma says so. What's that noise?"

John turned his gaze toward the sky. A humming noise, and a good deal of loud screeching filled the air.

"It's the cursed pigeons," John answered. "They've come back early this year and they're lookin' for food from the air. Let's get this sap down the hill fast."

Pulling and tugging the heavy sled over the muddy snow as best they could, the boys hurried along. They looked up to see what seemed to be a passing cloud. The sun was darkened for a moment, as thousands of birds flew over them. By now the screeching was so loud they had to cover their ears. With his heart pounding in his ears, John pulled the dazed William forward. "Keep movin'. They won't hurt you!" he shouted.

"I'm scared, John. What if they think we're trees and land on us?"

"They won't if we keep movin'." The pigeons began to settle into nearby trees. "Anyway, we're down the hill and

7

the sugarin' camp is right here." The two shaken boys pulled the sled into a clearing. There, standing in a cloud of wood smoke and steam, a slender Indian woman calmly stirred pots over an open fire. Beside her, feeding the fire, was John's friend Noah. Other Indians came and went, emptying buckets they had gathered and talking with friends.

"Hello, John Conner. Why did you come in running? I did not know we were racing to the sugar camp," said Noah to his friend.

"I was scared of the pigeons," William said, trying to pull one of the heavy buckets off the sled. Noah's mother was stirring two pots, one that had been cooked for many hours and was almost boiled down to sugar, another that was just starting, with thin sap cooking in it. The sap the Conner brothers were bringing needed to go into the "thin syrup" pot.

"In the spring and fall there are so many pigeons. They always give me a fright. I don't think I like spring," William Conner said.

"Ah, young ones, do not be afraid of pigeons," Rebecca said, reaching to help him with his buckets. "Those *maw-maws* are not interested in having you for their night meal. They are looking for the groves of nut trees." John took the last two buckets to the steaming syrup pot. Noah took the long spoon from his mother and began to stir the pot.

Rebecca went on without looking at the boys. "This flock is as nothing compared to the one I saw many seasons ago in Smoky Moon. I was out in the dry fields, gathering the last of the runner beans. I heard the great noise of gathering birds. A great black mass flew over my head. They kept coming and coming until I could not see the sun. Their flapping wings beat against each other so closely some fell to earth, pecked at and pushed out."

8

John looked up at her with respect in his eyes. She was a woman he trusted, the mother of the Delaware playmate he liked so well.

"The ways of God, the Great Spirit, are many and wonderful," Rebecca went on. "Birds are special winged messengers from Him, and they are good friends. Did you know that my Lenape name was Birdsong?"

John nodded. He knew that when an Indian was baptized by the missionaries, he or she received a Christian name. Noah used to be Running Wolf, but when his family came to the mission, he was given the name Noah from the Bible.

"The Lord sends the *maw-maws* to give us food for the night meal. Now that I am a Christian, I say, 'Thank the Lord for his goodness.' We must not question his ways."

John nodded, but William frowned. "I still do not like the pigeon time," he said.

Rebecca went on, "William, you do not really fear the spring. You know you are glad when the harshness of winter

9

is over. The seasons come and go and bring their changes, and it is well they do. Flowers die and re-bloom. Birds fly away in winter and return when earth re-awakens. Change is the way of Nature."

But William still did not look happy. "When will the noise end, Rebecca?" he asked.

"They roost and rest now," said the Indian woman. "Soon they will answer the call of their empty stomachs."

The two copper kettles were boiling merrily over the fire. "If you wait a few moments, something good will come to you. This kettle is almost ready to make candy," the Indian woman said.

John and William sat cross-legged by the fire talking to Noah and some of the other Delawares. "It seems to take all day to boil down," John thought. Because he had been waiting so long for it, this candy should taste extra good.

The missionaries were trying to teach the Indians easier ways of doing things. They had cows and chickens in this new village, where the Indians lived in hewn log cabins with chimneys instead of flimsy shelters with smoke holes in their bark roofs. Rebecca was trying a better way to make creamier maple candy. She had already skimmed the surface of the syrup. Now she poured in milk and whites of eggs from the chickens they were learning to raise.

"Come get your candy, young ones," Rebecca said, as she finally poured out thick syrup onto the snow. It made dark, tasty loops that quickly hardened into candy for the boys to pick up.

"And that is not all. You will see that he who is patient in life gets rewards. Here is something good from the syrup pot too." She carried dried gourd dippers to the pot, one for each of the boys. John and William were licking their fingers and lips as they left the clearing.

As the boys walked back to their cabin, they heard a great whooping sound and rush of air. As fast as they had come,

10

the birds had gone. John and William looked at each other with relief.

At supper that night there was cold wild turkey, shot by Richard Conner, their father, with his Kentucky rifle. There were corn cakes, the last of the shrivelled potatoes left in the "winter hole" in the floor of the cabin, and crabapple sauce. But best of all was sliced mush with the good, new maple syrup.

John sighed as he thought of the work that had gone into making the mush. His father had told him that the far-away white settlements had grinders and even great mills to grind the hard corn kernels. Here in New Schoenbrunn they must pound the grains into "samp" with a stump mortar—a piece of wood stuck in a hollowed-out log. Someday, Reverend Zeisburger said, the mission would be settled in enough to have a real water mill.

How nice it would be to have all the mush he wanted without having to use a hand grinder, John Conner thought. He wondered again what it would it be like to live like a white man. He thought of the tales his father had told, of the big city near where he had been brought up, of horse carriages and tall houses, and stores to buy anything you wished. But Richard Conner had turned his back on the cities. He had chosen to live with tribes in the wilderness, because he liked them, and their freedom.

Later that evening the boys were tucked in their beds upstairs in the cabin's loft. They drifted off to sleep watching the lights from the fireplace hearth below dance across the log timbers. John Conner could hear his parents' quiet whispers drifting up the rope ladder into the loft hole. They were talking about the war.

"British don't want us here..." "...try to break up this mission because we keep these Delawares in our village from fighting." "...maybe send the Shawnees on the rampage against us."

11

John Conner rolled over and thought, "'Tis a time of change for us all." He fell asleep with an uneasy feeling in the pit of his stomach.

Chapter Two

Captured by Warring Indians

New Schoenbrunn, where the Conners lived, was not the only Moravian mission village in the Ohio Country. There were two others: Gnadenhutten and Salem. The Delawares and missionaries who lived there were pledged not to fight in the Revolutionary War, but the missions were very exposed to the troubles of that war.

13

As the Revolution drew to a close and the British tried hard to win, their officers fought to hold Ohio Country. They suspected the white missionaries in the Moravian villages were helping the Americans, so they sent their fierce Indian allies to destroy the peaceful villages.

British soldier Matthew Elliot came leading Indians with fearful names: Half-King of the Wy-an-dots, Captain Pipe of the fighting Delawares and John and Thomas Snake of the Shawnees.

All were suspicious of the peaceful Delaware Indians in the Moravian villages because they would not join the war.

On September 4, 1781, while it was still dark, young John Conner snuggled further down under the woven rabbit skin blanket on his bed. He felt cozy and warm there, as the rain pounded down on the oak shakes that served as shingles above his head. The wind whipped through some of the cracks in the logs, but for the most part his father had wedged in enough wooden strips to keep the water out.

He was just drifting back off to sleep when a frightening yell sounded through the rainy dawn. "Awe-OHHHHH." It was the Indian scalp yell.

The front door crashed open. Three Wyandot warriors with painted faces charged in. John's older brother James didn't seem too afraid, but John and William were! Downstairs two of the Indians yanked the fur robe off his parents' bed in the corner and dragged them to the door. Baby Henry, rudely awakened by his mother's side, began to cry.

When John saw an Indian with a war-painted face and strange hair looking fiercely up into the loft, his heart skipped a beat. These were not at all like the Delaware friends he knew! James, John and William grabbed for their trousers as they were herded down the ladder.

One of the Indians screamed another scalp yell. Similar yelps came in answer from all across the village. Now all four of the boys began to cry. The little family was pushed out into the soaking rain. As they slipped about on the mud,

14

Indians closed in to prod them with rifle butts and knife points.

John was more afraid than he had ever been in his life. The prisoners from New Schoenbrunn were pushed along the road towards Gnadenhutten. When they arrived at this village, they saw hundreds of other prisoners being huddled into one group.

All the missionaries and Christian Indians from the three Moravian towns were prisoners of the British and their native allies. The sun, coming through the mist and the last of the rain, gave them little comfort.

John saw that his friend Noah and Noah's mother Rebecca had been captured too. "Christian Indian," a Wyandot said to Noah and kicked the boy's leg.

The next few days passed in a haze of confusion for six-year-old John Conner. All the Indians were rough with him and his family, kicking them about, refusing to shelter them, throwing food at them at mealtime. Only the Delawares were decent to the prisoners.

The Wyandot Indians were the worst. Some of them wore clothing they had stolen from the cabins in the Moravian villages. They were strutting about like proud roosters.

When James, the oldest Conner boy, saw one warrior prancing about with his own felt slouch hat on, he was very angry.

Finally the prisoners were allowed to build leanto shelters and fires for warmth and cooking.

Margaret Conner paced through the grass. She carried Baby Henry on a native cradle board. "I wonder how my garden is doing," she said to John, who walked behind her to try to dig some roots for the supper pot.

"I worked hard on the corn and beans and the herb patch. Some of the cows and hogs ran from the Wyandots into the woods. I suppose they are eatin' everything in sight."

15

John Conner was worrying about more than that. He was wondering where the Wyandots would take his family.

On September 11, he found out. All four hundred Moravian Indians and missionaries, and the Conners too, were brought together at Salem for a trip into the unknown wilderness.

With Wyandot warriors guarding and threatening them, all these folk left the missions behind and went into the woods. They also left behind gardens full of fat vegetables, corn and pigs. Hunger would be a part of the lives of the Conner family for many weeks to come.

The group was split in two. Some went in canoes on the river, others walked, driving a huge herd of cattle northward. The family of Richard Conner went by land, with Mrs. Conner carrying Baby Henry on her back in the cradle board, and Mr. Conner carrying first William, then John. James walked as best he could up the bumpy, awful trail.

Most of the prisoners, of course, were Christian Indians who had been living at the Moravian missions. Noah and his mother Rebecca and the rest were treated rather well by their captors. But the few white people who were in the group were bothered and tormented. The Indians slapped their legs and pushed slow people aside, leaving them to die by the road.

Margaret Conner dressed her family completely in Indian fashion, so they would not stand out and thus ask for more torment.

"We do look as Indians," she whispered to her husband. It was easy for the father and mother because they had lived among Indians so long their language and body movements were like the red men's. And the older Conner boys, James, John and William, were dark-haired. But baby Henry's hair was as white as straw. There was no mistaking that he was white.

Kicking an old lead ball out of the dirt with her shoe as she walked along, Margaret Conner got an idea.

"John, come here quick, I say." "Take the lead ball and
rub it between your hands. But keep walking."

John did as he was told, wondering what his mother was
up to.

"Let me see your hands now," she said. John held his
hands out and showed her the black palms.

"Good," she said. "Now come around to the cradle board
and as I bend down, rub your hands all over Henry's head."

"But Ma," John said, "He'll get all black. . ."

"Shh, that's the point," Margaret answered. "Now be fast
about your work."

Rebecca, walking silently behind with Noah, smiled. She
knew what Margaret Conner planned.

John wiped his dirty hands all over Henry's face and hair,
and the black lead turned it darker and darker. The baby
giggled with delight. Margaret looked at her baby, hoping
she would soon have time to unwrap his buckskin blanket

17

and change the diaper of tree moss he wore. She continued down the trail with a family who now looked all Indian.

Later that day the captive party arrived at the forks of the Mus-king-um River. The Wyandot warriors began bragging that they would hunt enough meat for the night-meal, even for the captives.

John Conner understood several Indian languages. He listened as one young boy told another, "One in our group has a tame buffalo cow near here. It feeds with the other cattle. Let us find and kill it." John pretended not to hear.

He and William followed the young warrior boys, some not much older than they, to the stream where the buffalo cattle drank.

The boys snickered as one called "Brave Warrior" stood up and shot the trusting animal.

That night, the Wyandots dined on buffalo hump, throwing the less tender parts of the animal to the captives.

"We are brave hunters of the Wyandot tribe," said the young warrior who had shot the buffalo.

"Brave you are to shoot a cow in a pasture," yelled John Conner, before his father pulled him away into the shelter of the trees.

The group trudged on. Some went by river as before and others by land. Soon they came to White Woman's Creek. A very weary Conner family settled in for another night on the trail. Their tired sleep was interrupted by a huge downpour of rain and crashing thunder.

"Up, everyone, up quick!" Richard Conner called to his sleeping family, rousing them as lightning lit the horizon.

Just then there was a loud crack. An oak tree crashed down where they had just been sleeping. Fat drops of rain pounded down quickly, flooding the ground. Mr. Conner tied a hemp rope around his own waist. Then he attached it to the older boys. He didn't want them to be swept away in the knee-deep water. Rain beat against the boys and their father, soaking their torn clothes, tossing them to and fro.

18

"I can hardly stand up, Pa," John wailed.

"Hang on, Margaret," Richard shouted through the roaring wind. Margaret Conner clutched the baby close to her chest, staring in horror at the trees crashing about them. The family huddled together for warmth and protection.

When daylight came, many roots of downed trees stuck up all around them. "We are alive," Mrs. Conner murmured, "Thank the Blessed Savior."

"Yes, thanks to Him, who has brought us so far, we do yet survive," said Richard Conner. "He must intend good works for me and my sons," he said. "May we be spared to bless his name!"

On October 1, when the captives reached the Sandusky River, their awful journey ended. Their feet were cut and blistered because they had been barefooted the last two days.

"Here you will stay," the Wyandots' Half-King said. With no other word of explanation, he turned to leave. He spat on the ground, in the style of the white man. "So much for those who help the Americans," he said. The group was abandoned. Over the next few days the sad, weak little group found a site and began to build a town which was later named Captives Town.

Chapter Three

White Indians in Michigan

The winter of 1781-1782 was a bitter cold one for those who remained at Captives Town. Luckily, Richard Conner had decided to move his family to Lower Sandusky, where food could be found. Richard knew as long as his family stayed in Wyandot country, they wouldn't be taken prisoner again.

In 1782 the Indian war approached the Conners' safe home at Sandusky. Richard Conner heard that an American, Major William Crawford, was coming near them to punish the Wyandots, Shawnees and Sen-e-cas for their raids against Pennsylvania and Virginia settlers.

This was the last straw for Richard. He packed up his family and headed out of Ohio. It was the right decision again. Soon the Wyandots caught Crawford and did a terrible thing to punish him for his raid. During the raid, a militia officer serving under Major Crawford had massacred 96 unarmed, innocent Indians at the Moravian town of Gnadenhutten. Now the tribesmen blamed Crawford and burnt him at the stake. Indian warfare in Ohio had reached an awful point.

Once again the Conner family followed David Zeisberger, who was now in Detroit in Michigan Country. Brother David was preparing to build a new mission. The commander at Fort Lernoult at Detroit had agreed to let the missionaries farm a piece of land along the Huron river and many of the Conners Indian friends came to join him.

It was a bright summer day in 1782. A refreshing June breeze rippled across the harbor as the Conner family approached Brother David's new mission. Local French and English families, wearing brightly-colored clothes, strolled the edge of the bank nearby, enjoying the cool country air.

The Conners turned east down to the shipyards of the town, where the Moravians had a temporary house. The Christian Indians' wigwams were beside the missionaries' house. The Conners saw men, women, and children strolling the streets, beginning to stop near the Moravian settlement. Music, lovely and pure, was coming from behind a high fence around the settlement. John Conner smiled. The people of Detroit were listening to his Indian friends singing Moravian hymns inside. They were not used to such a thing in this town.

French and English children climbed high on shipyard crates to get a better view. "Ma, those Indians sing like angels," one little girl said to her mother. The Conners entered the temporary village, feeling right at home.

Soon, work began on the new, permanent mission twenty miles away. After a while, twenty-seven log houses stood on the sandy bluffs. This new Moravian mission village was named New Gnadenhutten.

Young John Conner, nine, and William, seven, felt comfortable and secure again. Here they settled, and here they spent the years at the close of the Revolutionary war.

"Snow, snow and more snow," John Conner thought. He gloomily lifted the wooden shutter to look out the window at five foot drifts. He had never seen so much snow.

"If my stomach didn't feel so empty, I could enjoy this sight more," he told himself. New Gnadenhutten was experiencing hard times. There was little food in this very cold winter of 1784. Even the deer had deserted the neighborhood. At times the Conners felt afraid of starving.

"We have learned to trust God," Margaret Conner said. "He will provide food." On this snowy day she had told the boys to try to play while their father struggled through the deep snow to go to the woods to hunt.

Even if he had the energy to play, John told himself, it would be hard to move in the drifts he was seeing outside the window. He heard the cows bumping the door, trying to keep warm. William joined him at the window.

"They keep lookin' at the river, John," he said, watching the poor, half-starved animals raise their heads and bellow, their breath making little clouds in the cold air.

"Maybe they are just thirsty," John said. "Why don't we try melting some snow for them, Will? Too bad we can't give them food." The cows were in danger of starving, too, because there was no grass or hay.

So the two boys scooped out a large kettle of snow and hung it over the fire to melt. After it had melted, William carried the kettle outside to the cows. He set it down, and its warm bottom hissed as it hit the cold snow. The cows began to drink the water, but after a few slurps, their noses sniffed the air again. John and Will were confused.

"What do they want? There's no food down there, more's the pity," John said. Looking down the path to the river, he saw his father slowly make his way back to the cabin. "Will, he has a doe on the sledge. A herd must have come back to us! Venison steaks! Stew!"

By the door of the cabin Richard Conner slit open the deer's stomach and got ready to cut up the meat.

"Well, well!" Richard said as steam from the warm deer swirled about his head. "Look what we have here." Richard poked his knife through the deer's insides and scooped out what appeared to be a green ball.

"Scrub grass! I've been wonderin' what those deer have been livin' off of in this freezin' winter." Richard wiped the knife clean on his pants.

"Pa," William asked. "Could that be what the cows are sniffin' for? They keep wantin' something down there by the water."

"Poor hungry creatures," his father replied. "The only way to find out is to get them down there."

The rest of the afternoon was spent shoveling a pathway down to the river for the cows. Soon the cows were pawing under the snow to feed on the same scrub grass the deer had been eating.

"I think this may be the Lord's answer to how we and our Indian friends will get through the winter," Richard Conner said in a pleased way. "Grass has come up under a warm blanket of snow." Not only was there grass under the snow along the banks of the river, but also there were huge fields of it beside the river.

Wearing "rackets," a kind of a snow shoe, the Delawares at the mission and the Conner family were able to walk over the snow the next day to kill deer as they came to feed on the grass. Not only that, but they gathered up baskets full of scrub grass for the other animals at the mission. The cows and hogs ate it. Even chickens could gobble it, if it was cut into nuggets the size of a grain of corn.

Perhaps with full stomachs the small, black cows could produce the fresh milk John liked, he told himself. If there was milk, there could be butter. John's mouth watered as he dreamed of hot bread and biscuits dripping with butter. This new mission had a beehive oven and both whites and Indians had been baking. Last summer Mrs. Zeisberger had taught Margaret Conner how to bake kaffeekuchen (coffecake), and it had become John's favorite. Perhaps in the spring and summer there would be thick wedges of sour cherry pie or apple tart, and maple-sugared cranberries again. But for now, in this hard winter, pickled wild cucumbers and wild game would have to do. It was, at least, food.

James, John, William and little Henry spent the rest of that cold winter feeding the stock and making brooms, baskets, and bowls from the grass. In the spring they would take the things they made to Detroit for trading.

"I'll like visiting the store to sell the things we make," John Conner told his parents, as he squinted his eyes in the firelight, making baskets. "I promise you I'll help Pa get every penny we can, I can tell you that!"

For supper each night there was enough fish and nuts and venison from the deer herds which had returned for all to eat and be full. And happy noises from the cradle of the new addition to the family, Baby Susanna, brightened the dark winter evenings.

Finally spring came to the little settlement in Michigan, with summer fast behind. On a beautiful warm June evening, John and his Delaware friend Noah set out for a hunting trip. John hadn't had much practice shooting his new Kentucky rifle yet. Up until now, he hadn't been old enough, his father said, to shoot a long rifle. But now that he was almost ten, his father had bought him a rifle when they went into the Detroit store and told him he could hunt.

John looked at the boy by his side. Noah was twelve and a half. He seemed like a man of the world to John Conner.

The leaves of black walnut and elms rustled about the boys as they walked through the giant forest. Insects of every type buzzed above their heads, making the forest seem as though it were breathing. The ground was covered with thick thistle and nettles, and John began to believe the shadows were playing tricks on the his eyes.

All of a sudden something dropped from a tree and John jumped in his tracks and cried, "Snake! There's a blacksnake! Give me a stick, hurry!" He fumbled around the ground looking for something to club it with.

"Wait! Do not kill the black grandfather snake. You should never kill a snake if you do not have to," Noah shouted.

John slowly put down the stick and watched the enormous snake slink along towards the wild rose bushes near their feet.

"Why shouldn't I kill the cursed thing?" John asked.

"The snake is a spiteful and mean animal," Noah told him.

"If you were to kill him, all his snake brothers would know it and return to frighten you. Besides, the blacksnake is not harmful." He watched the snake slither away. "Blacksnake is more possum at heart than anything else."

But John's heart was still pounding. "If that had been a rattlesnake, I would have smashed him but good," he said. "Indian custom or not."

"A rattlesnake bite is bad," Noah told him, "but Delawares know how to heal it. One good way is to put on a poultice of crushed red elm leaves." John looked steadily at his Indian friend. After so many years together, he and Noah had been separated after the march. Noah had returned to relatives in a non-Christian village, but he and his mother had joined the mission again when Brother David had called them back. Now both Rebecca's and Richard Conner's families were living at New Gnadenhutten.

"You need to learn more of the woodland ways of the Delawares, John Conner," Noah said. "You know much because your mother lived with our people, but you must learn more than the corn hoeing she can teach you. You say you like Indian ways, but what you are learning here is to eat bread from the bakery ovens. Do you wish to learn to be a Delaware?"

John nodded eagerly, and his friend went on. "When a Delaware is ready to become a man, at ten or eleven like you, an older man teaches him the Indian ways of survival. While I was back with my people, my uncle taught me. Now I will be your uncle."

John Conner's eyes danced in excitement. Since he had seen Detroit, he no longer yearned so much to live in the city. The stores were wonderful, but the rest of the town was such a dirty, falling-down little village! Lately everything about his Indian friends fascinated him. "Teach me the secrets of the woods, Noah," he insisted.

The Delaware boy was leaning against a huge white walnut. "The spirit of the great walnut sends his help to us in many disguises. We only need to look," he told his new pupil. "This bark can soothe many wounds—the pounding head, the throbbing tooth, even the gash from the claw of a bear. These will all be eased by the bark of this tree." He

26

pulled off a piece of bark and handed it to John. Then he went around to the north side of the tree.

"On cloudy days when you are on an unknown course, you can watch the great trees for moss. More moss grows on the north side of the tree than the south. If you cannot follow the sun, follow the moss. And if you bleed, quickly pick some moss, put it in the stream and stick it on the wound. It will help congeal the blood."

He walked to where wild grape vines hung down almost to the ground. "Dry the fruit of this vine and put it on boils and poison ivy leaf rash. And chestnut leaves—they are good for cough. Do not forget. Coughs come often around the low rivers in the summertime in this place of Michigan." As they walked the trail, Noah pointed out more Indian healing plants, some of which John already knew. May Apple for stomach pains, white oak for burns—his mother had taught him these simple ones.

John Conner said, "At least I know how to set fishin' traps. That I learned long ago."

The two boys reached the edge of the creek where they had set out "weirs," or traps used for catching fish. John put his rifle down on the grass and peered over the edge.

"Looks like this trap can sit for another day," he said holding up one of the baskets. "It can hold a lot more fish."

"How can you tell, John?" Noah said, laughingly. "You need to look beneath the water." He had come up behind John and now ducked him playfully, pushing his head under the water.

Sputtering and choking, John pulled his head up. He didn't enjoy the joke. "Why did you have to go and do that for?" he cried in Delaware. He began shaking from the cold water dripping down his body.

"You are a girl-baby. Do not be a weakling! You will have to do better if you are to be a true Delaware," his friend said and then, more kindly, helped him dry his hair

27

off. "Now come, if we are going night-hunting, we must prepare the torch. It's starting to get dark."

Their canoe, a beautiful one made from a poplar log, was
lying beneath a clump of tall reeds. It had been hollowed
out by burning and was tapered at each end. The boys
turned the canoe over and pulled out its one-bladed paddle.
Then they looked for the hickory bark torch which had been
snugly stored underneath the canoe in a deerskin pouch.
Good! It was still clean and dry.

Noah began the hard task of lighting the torch with his
flint rock. Then he climbed with it into the canoe and the
two boys glided over the smooth water. The moon cast an
eerie glow over them. Noah sat at the back of the canoe,
paddling and steering, while John was in the front holding
the torch with one hand. In the other was his gun.

"Keep your eyes open," Noah commanded from the back
of the canoe. "The bucks and their wives love to come to the

river's edge at night to eat. There the biting flies do not bother them."

"Shh, I see something," John said.

Noah pulled the paddle out of the water and the canoe slowed down.

"Look, over by that fallen tree," said the Indian boy. "There is the first deer you will shoot with the new rifle." Very quietly, very slowly, they paddled straight for the deer. John held the torch up high and Noah started to rock the canoe. The deer stood still, looking into the glaring light of the torch. He was completely hypnotized.

The canoe drifted a few feet forward and John felt dizzy. Through the flickering torch light, as the canoe rocked, the deer looked like some huge monster! John squinted and remembered his eyes could be playing tricks on him. He tightened his grip on the new rifle and got ready to make his move.

He leaned the torch against the "V" of the canoe. The deer's eyes were glued to the torch. John put powder into the flash pan, cocked the hammer, aimed, and squeezed the trigger. The shot echoed across the water, and the backfire almost sent the torch over the side of the canoe.

"Fine aim, my friend," Noah shouted. "Let's go get her." A good sized doe was lying across a log up on shore. The canoe ground across sand and the boys jumped out.

John held the torch up to the deer to see if it was dead. There was no sign of life; he had shot from close range.

"Roll her over on her side and hold her," John said to Noah. "I'll gut her so we can get the carcass into the canoe."

John pulled out his short knife from the deerskin sheath which hung around his neck. Although he had watched his father many times, he hesitated. "Cut carefully, right up the middle of the belly," Noah told him.

The insides of the deer ran onto the ground. "Hold the torch closer, Noah. I need to find the heart and liver for Ma. She makes good stews from 'em."

29

Insects were beginning to swarm over the insides as John quickly picked through for the heart and liver.

"I offer you half the catch, as Delaware custom decrees," John said proudly, as they lugged the deer to the Conner cabin.

They hung the deer up by its head from a tree overnight to let the rest of the blood drain out.

The next morning Noah came to get his venison and help clean the deerskin. He gave it to Mrs. Conner for tanning.

Then the Delaware boy said to John, "Come with me, my friend. There is something I must do for you. And bring your brother Will. From now on, he will be my friend, too."

William Conner's eyes were wide as Noah took him and John into an abandoned bear cave near the camp. "What you have learned from me and the other Delawares, John Conner, you can pass on to your brother Will. Today I make you both my blood brothers."

He took out sharp fishbones and reached for John's bare arm. William stared as he watched Noah prick a circle of holes, drawing blood in each.

"Ouch," John started to say, but closed his mouth. A Delaware does not cry out, no matter what the pain.

"I have drawn the deer of our hunt on your arm. It is your protecting animal. All animals are given to man as gifts of the Great Spirit; we hunt them fairly and freely to survive. They understand we must find and kill them."

He took poplar bark powder and rubbed it over the line of pricks in John's arm. "I think you will always hunt well, John Conner."

"Now, William Conner." Will did not flinch when Noah took his arm and pricked the drawing until its shape was outlined in blood.

Noah sat back. "There, he said, "I have tattooed a wolf cub to remind you of my Delaware clan, William Conner." He smiled, almost to himself and looked at their new tattoos.

"Now you are both Delaware—almost," he said.

"I don't want to be anything else but an Indian, ever," said William, awe-struck.

"I don't think I know how to be anything else BUT an Indian," John Conner thought, trying not to rub his stinging arm.

Chapter Four

White Indians in Indiana

The Conner family finally had to part from their Indian
and Moravian friends in 1786. New Gnadenhutten didn't
become the religious center Zeisberger had hoped it would.
Only a small number of converts arrived, and the O-jib-was
weren't interested in Christianity. Detroit merchants bought
the mission for $400. Zeisberger led his Indians south to
Ohio.

Richard and Margaret Conner decided not to go with their missionary friends, and the young Conner brothers, William and John, spent the rest of their childhood living in Michigan. Since the family loved Indian life, they went to be with the Ojibwas. The boys' father, Richard, began farming land in what is now Macomb County and built his family a log house. They still spent a good deal of time with Indians, hunting, fishing and trapping animals.

The few other white people who lived in the area where John and William grew to be young men, thought the Conners were different. "They talk, live and dress like Indians," they said.

John and William Conner were what some people on the frontier called "White Indians." These were men who chose to live among the Indians for one reason or another. They spoke the Indian tongue, they dressed in leggings and breechclout. They stayed out in the weather and sun, so their skin was dark and tough like an Indian's.

Richard and Margaret Conner stayed in Michigan the rest of their lives. James, Susanna and Henry went their own ways, but John and William felt close to each other, even after they grew up.

Both John and William spoke many languages: they may have spoken English, German, three types of Delaware, Shawnee, Ojibwa and some Wyandot. When 1800 came, John Conner entered into fur trading south in the territory of Indiana. He believed he could buy furs and sell goods to most of the tribes in the West.

William Conner, too, eventually decided to leave the family home and follow John. He knew about the signing of the Greenville Treaty, which set aside land just for Indians in Indiana Territory. Since he thought of himself as a white Indian, he wanted to trade, and while he was at it, to seek out his Indian friends.

The tribe he loved most were the Delawares. Some of William's long-ago Ohio friends had settled along the west

33

branch of the White River in Indiana. His brother John must be with them, and he wasn't the only one. Noah might be in one of those villages, too!

It would be nice to see his friends again, William told himself. He had learned a good deal about trading from the French in Michigan, and he could do business here in Indiana with the Delawares.

William arrived at the village named Wap-i-mins-kink (Chestnut Tree Place) on a cool fall evening. This was the home of Chief William Anderson and his band of Delawares. He would look for his old friends here. Chief Anderson was said to be a smart and fair Indian, and William wanted to meet him.

"Have a seat," Chief Anderson said as he pointed at a bench. The seat looked more like a platform. William was used to sitting on such benches in Delaware Council houses.

The seat was along the log wall, one foot above the ground and five feet across. It looked like a big bed. First it had been covered with tree bark and then with long pieces of grass to make it softer to sit or lie on.

"You come among us looking and talking like one of us, yet you have the skin of a white man. You speak perfect Delaware, yet your eyes say you have no tribal blood. You are a strange one. The whites want us to become more like them, yet you want to be like us!" the chief said.

William didn't speak. He knew he should be quiet until the chief asked him to speak. In the center of the roomy lodge a pretty Indian girl with dark, shiny eyes was stirring a large kettle. The kettle hung over a fire. Soon she ladled out large helpings of steaming corn and boiled venison into a wooden bowl and carried them to Chief Anderson and William.

William nodded in thanks and watched the pretty young woman take a bowl for herself and sit down beside the kettle.

"Her name is Me-king-es," Chief Anderson said, "and she is under my protection. She is a large-hearted girl and a

34

hard worker, too. Not so her brother." Chief Anderson pointed to a sleeping Indian brave huddled in the corner.

"White man's whisky has its claws in him. He hunts skins only to sell to traders for whisky, while his family goes hungry." He had finished his bowl of venison and set it on the ground.

William put down the bowl of stew and wiped his mouth on the back of his sleeve.

"My first task is to find my brother. I knew if anyone had heard of him, it would be you. His name is John Conner. He was going to meet the French trader Pilkey," he said.

"No, I do not know your brother John, but I do know this French trader you speak of. We do not like him. Your brother should stay far from him, I tell you.

"Not all traders are bad at heart, but he is. It pains my spirit to see the unfair ways he treats our people. He sells fancy red and blue cloth and bright silk ribbons to our women. Then they worship the trader's cloth and cannot live without more. They do not make their own clothing from skins anymore. Soon they will forget how.

"The men trade for rifles and gun powder at unfair rates. They cannot repair the guns when they break down, as they often do. Pilkey sells much whisky and it makes the evil spirits go into our young men. I fear my people will forget the customs of the Old Ones and I blame him and others like him. We have travelled so far. We cannot forget who we are."

William stretched out on the wooden platform. Chief Anderson handed him a pipe and the two of them smoked in a friendly way together for a long time as smoke ascended upward in the lodge to please the spirits. William thought about what Chief Anderson was saying.

He knew it was true the Delawares had travelled far. The Delaware Indians had been pushed slowly westward since the first settlers had come to America in the 1600's. The Delawares moved west first from New Jersey to Pennsylvania.

35

Then, when whites wanted that land, the Delawares had to go to Ohio. This is where William knew them.

Now they were even pushed out of Ohio and were living here in Indiana on land given them by the Pi-an-ke-shaw Indians. They wanted to live in peace on land that would be always theirs.

The whites had made them give up their land, but they could not make them give up their customs. They were a hunting people, with a great love for the woodlands.

Would the Delawares give up their hunting ways now that whites were moving even into Indiana? It was easier to use white man things. Hunting was easier with a rifle. Cooking was better in an iron kettle.

Now, since treaties had been signed, the government was telling them to learn to farm. Would they do it? The Christian Delawares in Ohio had learned a little farming when they were with David Zeisberger, but even they didn't like it very much. Would these Indians ever change and become farmers? William didn't know.

He asked about his friends among the Christian Delawares.

"There are a few of them here," Chief Anderson said. He told William that Noah was in one of his other villages, Buck-on-ga-he-las Town up the river a little bit.

"My old friend! I will try to see him while I am here," William said.

"Tomorrow we will hold our Big House Ceremony, Conner. You may stay and watch. It is time to honor our protecting manitto, the Great Spirit. You will see I mean to keep our customs alive. Without them my people will forget who they are and will die! Mekinges will show you where you sleep."

With that William stood up and nodded respectfully at the chief. He followed the young Indian woman Mekinges out into the crisp, fall evening to find a cabin to sleep in.

36

William stretched his legs the next morning and took a walk around Chestnut Tree Town. He saw the usual log huts along the river. Overhead were large oaks, sycamores and chestnut trees in full fall color.

William's moccasins rustled through the red and orange leaves as he walked over to a small group of Indian boys playing nearby. "They're playing the bowl game—cherry stone—that Noah and John and I used to play," thought William.

"I caught four times this turn," one Indian boy shouted.

"Now it's your turn." The boy handed the wooded bowl holding six cherry pits to his friend. Some of the seeds were painted black, some yellow. The object of the game was to see how many small cherry pits you could catch in three turns. Whoever caught the most pits, won.

"There, I'm done," said the second boy. "I only caught three." He sighed. "I guess you win." Then he saw William and said to him, "Do you want to play?"

William bounced the pits about a little, laughing. "Indian children are so free," he thought. It was one of the reasons he had liked to be with them, not wearing tight "neckstock" collars and reading from books the way white men did.

As he walked through the village he spied Mekinges shooing a cow out of her garden. He hurried to help her.

The morning sun gently touched the top of her head, sending shimmering streaks of light through the dark ponytail.

"Can I help you?" William asked, and picked up a stick to herd the cow out of the garden.

"Yes, I just can't seem to keep them away from the corn," Mekinges said, flicking the ponytail about.

"We take these cows and pigs the white man thinks we should have, but our men don't seem to care about them. They won't build fences to keep them from eating the vegetables. Then they wonder why there is no squash to feed their stomachs. Heavy hoofs make ruined crops," she sighed.

37

William watched Mekinges as she stood there shaking her head over the trampled cornstalks and pumpkin vines. "What a pretty girl she is," he thought. "There is something special about her."

"I know the Great Spirit will be angry if we give up native custom, but surely a fence or two wouldn't anger him," she said as she threw the trampled pumpkins and squash into the bushes.

"My brother, Walks Straight, says that every time one of us gives up something Indian to become more like whites, we get a sickness. The Great Spirit becomes angry. Walks Straight should know! He has ruined his special name from his quest-in-the-woods when he was a boy. He can't walk straight any more because of white man's whisky!"

She looked up at William with pain in her eyes, and he nodded kindly. "Walks Straight says he is being punished," Mekinges said. "He says the Great Spirit took away his newborn son. What do you think Conner? Does the Great Spirit punish us for using the things of the white man?"

"Not all things of the white man are good, Mekinges," William Conner told her. "Believe me, I know. His towns and cities, like Detroit, are dirty and ugly places. I would like to think the Creator would let us live together in peace, perhaps take the best of each. Appreciate each other for what we are. 'Specially since what YOU are is lovely, Mekinges," William said.

The Delaware girl smiled and walked off towards the river.

William spent the day relaxing around the Indian village and asking if anyone knew his brother, John. One of the Delawares who had come in for the Big House Ceremony, finally told him "I do know your brother. He has just come into Buckongahelas Town."

"Ah, I will see him tomorrow, and Noah too!"

As evening approached, Indians could be seen coming in and out of the Big House getting ready for tonight's ceremo-

38

ny. The Delawares called it the Gam-wing. William had never seen one of these ceremonies, for the Christian Delawares in the missionary villages did not do them, thinking they were pagan.

The Delawares believed in twelve "deities" or spirit-gods. The spirit with the most power was Number Twelve, and as you went down each one had less and less power. Number One had the least power.

This lowest god, Number One, walks the earth and is invisible. He watches what people are doing and reports it to Number Two spirit each day. The report then keeps travelling on until it reaches the highest spirit, Number Twelve.

The Big House Ceremony honors all twelve spirits. In it the Indians give thanks to the spirits for the gifts of nature. The festival is held for twelve days and nights, one for each spirit. This was night one.

William had reached the long house. He came in, quietly took a seat, and looked around him. The long house was about forty feet long and twenty feet wide. It was made out of split logs set together between dug-in posts. The roof was made of tree bark.

He noticed that both ends of the house were open with no door to them. There were fires going inside, one at each end. He looked up to see openings in the roof above each fire to let the smoke escape.

Groups of men and women were sitting in their own rows around a center post. On the center post faces were carved on the east and west side. William noticed the wrinkles on the carved faces, which made the faces look old and wise. This center post wasn't the only carved post in the lodge. There were ten others.

"Of course," he thought. "Twelve faces for twelve spirits." A woman they called Ash-kah-suk, ceremonial helper, finished her twelfth sweep of the dirt floor with her turkey wing brush.

Chief Anderson stood up and began to shake a land-turtle shell. "The way those pebbles rattle around inside the shell makes a good rhythm," William thought. He had heard them before, in Ohio. Everyone stood up, so William did too. He listened as the chief began to speak.

"In my childhood I had a dream. In this dream I was setting a raccoon trap, and the trap snapped back and bit into my hand like a hungry bear. Just then a great white owl landed on a branch next to the raccoon trap. The owl promised to help me if I would obey him whenever he came to me. I promised, and he released my swollen hand from the trap with the flap of his wing. Now the white owl is my special protector."

After Chief Anderson was done telling his dream, the rest of the Indians repeated it all together word for word.

"I heard the owl's voice singing," Chief Anderson continued. He began to sing.

Two men near the back began beating on folded deerskin drums with flat sticks. Human heads were carved into the end of the sticks. The drums made a dull, thudding sound. Chief Anderson stopped singing, and William watched in surprise as all the Indians beside him did twelve jumps in a row in a sort of dance.

Then Anderson started his dream all over again and William began to understand what was happening. In fact, William even thought HE could see the white owl of the chief's dream. What an odd feeling!

As the story went on, William turned his head a bit. He jumped slightly. Red, glassy eyes glowed through the smoky darkness at him. Something—was it a huge animal?—stood up and started towards him. Big, snarling teeth and huge, furry claws seemed to be coming at the row of men. William's heart pounded as the bear thing came towards him. Then William smiled. He saw it was an Indian dressed in bearskins.

41

This bear Indian moved towards a brave in the corner and jabbed him with a pointed stick. The young brave had been joking around with his friend. No one could joke at the Big House ceremony! It was serious. The bear-Indian was in charge of keeping everybody serious.

Twelve Indians who had been given wam-pum (beads of polished purple and white shells strung in strands) were outside howling loudly. They sang their howl song twelve times, so he knew they must be making prayers to the twelve spirits.

As the evening continued, more Indians told their dreams. The wind blew outside; the fire burned. Honest, good faces were all around him. The sound of the Delaware language was on every lip, and he understood it so well. William began to feel as if he were home at last, among the Delawares.

"I never feel this way when I am among white men," he thought.

The next day, William went to Buckongahelas Town for a happy reunion with his brother John and their friend Noah. With John he talked of starting a trading partnership. With Noah he talked of old times and boyhood pranks.

When William asked about Rebecca, Noah's mother, the Indian looked sad. "My mother died when fever came four years ago. I miss her. A lot has changed since I last saw you, my friend."

William was glad to see his brother and old friend doing well. Noah was in the business of trapping fur animals, John in the business of trading them.

"I do not have time to go to the woods for fun, as we used to," Noah said. "I have a wife now." He smiled mysteriously. "It takes all my time to get the cooking pots and white man's cloth she wants." Then he grew serious. "I have changed my name. I have taken back my Delaware name of Running Wolf. I no longer follow the ways of the Moravians."

William could not help but look at the tattooed wolf cub, faint but still able to be seen, on his arm.

"Oh, you think I have changed, my friend, do you?" Running Wolf said, smiling at William. "Well, let me tell you the Great Spirit's law. It is that here on earth all things change. I seem to remember my mother told us all that once. But I do not wish them to change much more. It will hurt the tribal peoples if they do." There was something angry in his voice.

John clapped his brother on the back. "And so, if you go into business here in Indiana with me, where will you settle? Will, there's lots of opportunity here. Will you stay here with me?"

John had left the bad French trader Pilkey and decided to open a post and store of his own at Buckongehelas Town.

"No, I am thinking of settlin' and tradin' at Chief Anderson's Chestnut Tree Village," William said. "Maybe I have a change or two to make myself."

Within a few days William returned to Chestnut Tree Town. He found a way to talk to Mekinges again. She was pounding cloth on a rock by the stream, doing her weekly wash.

"My brother gave me some white man's lye soap," William said, handing her a creamy cake of hard soap. "It should make your job easier."

"Let us hope I do not get a sickness too, as my brother says, from these white man's things," Mekinges told him with a smile.

He watched her a long while. "You are not married," he said finally.

"I have never found a man among the tribesmen whom I could respect. Many have come bearing gifts to my relatives to show that they wish me for wife. But I do not respect them and that is most important for man and wife of all things." There was a sparkle in her eye and the hint of a smile.

43

"And if a man like me sent presents to your relatives' hut to ask for you? Could you respect a man like that?"

"Perhaps. But that man would not be an Indian."

"No," said William, "but he would be a white Indian, speak Delaware tongue, hunt as a Delaware, obey sacred customs."

"We shall see. White Indians are not Indians, though they may think they are. But we shall see."

Chapter Five

Conner Store and Trading Post

It was the year 1803. William Conner was happily settled in a new log home with his wife Mekinges. Their double log cabin was four miles south of what is today Noblesville, Indiana. There was a Delaware Indian town nearby.

After Mekinges and William had married and left Anderson's Chestnut Tree Town, they had decided to claim this good stretch of land by the river for their home. William had had his eye on the land for a while. He had seen it several times as he scouted on horseback.

By building a cabin, he had given himself a claim on the land, and he told himself he would buy it later. Someday, he thought, it would be for sale. Already his cabin was being called "Conner Trading Post." He took in the furs Indians brought to him and gave them lead, flint, steel knives and hatchets. These trade goods he kept neatly arranged on shelves on one wall of the cabin.

"I think it's time we paid John a visit, don't you, Mekinges?" William said one day. "I would like to see his new store at Cedar Grove, and we need to talk about our fur trading partnership. He has married an Indian wife, too, and we should get to know her. Let's make a trip tomorrow."

Cedar Grove, where John lived, was in the valley of the Whitewater River, in eastern Indiana Territory. William and Mekinges mounted their horses to start out on the Indian path to Cedar Grove. The horses were packed lightly for this trip. Mekinges's silver-gray mare carried bedrolls and cooking pots, while William's horses was loaded with dried deer meat, corn meal and other food supplies.

William had his gun on his shoulder, his tomahawk slung at his side, and his knife around his neck.

"I still like to walk the trail whenever I can instead of going horseback," William told Mekinges. "I want to keep the trail skills Noah taught me sharp, and I like to live like the old Delawares did as often as I can." William knew that only recently did the woodland Indians use horses much for travelling. He spent a good deal of time hunting and setting fishing lines with men from the Delaware settlement near his cabin, and he loved to observe their customs as he had when he was a boy.

Sometimes William and Mekinges wore shoes, but for this trip they had decided to wear the traditional Indian moccasins. These soft, light moccasins would be comfortable when they reached John's new town. The only trouble with moccasins was that they got holes in them—they wore out. So the Conners had extra deerskin with them to make new ones if that happened.

It was a hard, slow trip for the horses through the thick beech and maple woods. Even from the height of the saddles, William and Mekinges were pricked by branches and slapped in the face by tree limbs. The couple made their way through what was sometimes dense underbrush crowded with blackberry and wild rose thickets. It was lucky they had on leather leggings. These protected their legs, and thick linen hunting shirts covered up their arms.

The ground was still soggy from rain the day before. Mekinges had to dismount and lead her horse over the swampy ground. "Wait, William, I'm stuck," Mekinges cried as she slipped in the mud. Her right leg sunk in up to her knee. William jumped down and grabbed her under both arms and yanked her out, As her foot came out, the mud slurped and ate up her moccasin.

"Grab it if you can, Mekinges," William shouted as he pointed to the hole where the moccasin had gone. "We don't want to take the time to make a new one."

Mekinges lay down on her stomach and stuck her arm in the thick mud to fish out the moccasin.

"We must make camp soon, William," she said, as she raised herself up. "Tonight there will be no moon to guide our path." She rinsed the muddy moccasin off in a little pool of water by the path and they carefully led the horses through boggy moss. Soon the trail began to clear up and they mounted the horses again, gratefully.

They went along the trail, looking at notches that had been placed in trees along the way, or sometimes bent sticks.

These "pointers" had been put there by other Indians travelling the same path. They helped mark the trail.

Mekinges and William followed along the banks of the river. The sun was starting to set. Soon large hills loomed up before them. The sun was almost down when William thought he spied part of a bark hut sticking out from behind a rock.

"Look, Mekinges," William said, as they reached the top of the hill and looked out over an open field burnt off by one of the prairie fires which sometimes hit. "I see the place we can camp for the night."

A hard-to-follow, tiny path led to a little cave under a rock ledge. There were two walls of bark coming out from the cave to give it extra protection from the wind.

The couple glanced down over the steep hill to the river below, and guided the horses down towards it. Soon they had tethered their mounts amidst a grove of small trees and had scurried into the safety of the shallow cave. A cold wind was beginning to blow against their backs.

"What's this, here?" William said to himself, pointing to one of the log posts holding up the wall. "J.C. 1802. Those are my brother's initials. I knew he had to have a hand in building this hut. It's just like ones we used to make when we lived in Michigan."

Mekinges went inside the cave-hut and unrolled the bearskin they were going to sleep on. She gathered up dry twigs and sticks and brushed aside a place in the dirt towards the edge of the ledge for a fire.

"We better get this fire started before the rains come," Mekinges said as she looked up at the cloudy sky.

They felt cozy and snug under their little ledge. It began to pour rain. The two bark sides kept the wind out, and by carefully rolling a few burning logs under the ledge, they could keep the fire going.

For dinner they cut off large chunks of the salted deer meat and broiled them over the fire. Then they fell asleep. They needed all the rest they could get for the remaining two day trip to Cedar Grove.

John Conner had left Buckongahelas Town earlier in the year. He had settled near Indian territory, in an area which a recent treaty had opened up to white settlers. He took his Indian wife with him, and he started a store which both settlers and Indians could use. At last he had a fine mercantile store like the ones he had admired as a boy!

William stood outside his brother's store at Cedar Grove. He noticed the finished look of it. "It doesn't look Indian," he thought, seeing the "puncheon" door made out of well-split logs.

"Well," he thought, as he went inside the store and saw his brother standing behind the counter. "John himself looks less like a Delaware—or any Indian, for that matter, than when I last saw him."

John Conner wore white man's linen trousers and had cut his hair. Perhaps it was going to the new capital city of Washington last year to interpret for a group of local Indians, and meeting Thomas Jefferson, that had changed John. It was true, William thought. His own brother had been asked to interpret for the President of the United States! He seemed different, but William knew he would still love and admire his brother.

John Conner looked up and came out from behind the counter. "Welcome, William, and sister-in-law. Come warm yourselves by my fire," John said and ushered them to the huge stone fireplace, where beech logs were blazing. William sat down on a small stool by the fire and Mekinges went to the corner where John's wife sat. Soon they were chatting happily in Delaware. Mekinges was glad John's wife was a tribal woman too.

"You are doing well, I see," said William as he glanced about the store. There was a counter with shelves above it, looking for all the world like a store in Detroit. There were packages of Barlow knives, sheep shears, farming tools. Farther down were dry goods, even a pickle barrel, and cracker tins, iron pots and pans, nice china dishes, and coffee and tea. Off to one side was a little table with a barrel of pure corn whisky.

"I'm glad you like my store. Pioneer settlers are comin' in now, and there are lots of Delawares and other tribal people nearby to trade with. It seemed like a good opportunity to make some money from both groups. And as I always said to the family, opportunity is m' middle name!"

"I remember that," William said, smiling. Men were coming in, heading for the whisky barrel.

"You're lookin' at the spirits, I see," John said heartily. "Whisky is sellin' fast."

"It always does," William murmured. Ever since he had come to know Mekingis's brother, Walks Straight, he had not liked seeing Indians drinking.

"I sell a lot of everything. Now that I'm located on government land, I don't need a license to sell."

"Governor Harrison is gettin' more land from Indian treaties all the time," William said.

"Yes," his brother replied. "Though I don't know if all of this treaty-makin' is really fair to the tribes, I can see the good things a white man's life has to offer."

William nodded.

"On my trip to Washington last year for Harrison, I saw so many fine things. Carriages, and window drapes, and even tubs to bathe in. I've been livin' among Indians so long I forget I really am white. I want some of those fine things."

Well! There really was a change here, William thought. "What was President Jefferson like?" he asked his brother.

"A man with many interests—readin', music, Indians too. He has so many good ideas for this land and so much more power than I ever imagined.

"I made some friends there, and I have found a better way to ship our furs out—through Washington," John went on. "Send me all the dress furs you can, Will, the highest quality, and I will send you trade goods. You can trade with the Indians where you are. We can make ourselves some real money."

"Well, we all need to live," thought William. "If I get fine skins and he sells them and makes a lot of money for us— well, I do have a family now."

Still, he told John firmly, "I don't mind making money, even plenty of it, but don't ask me to be part of what you call the civilized world. I'm not ready for that yet. You know I like the ways of the woods."

"No, I won't. But mind you, if you do this, I said first quality. Some of these furs go to England, and lords and ladies wear them."

William thought about that a moment. He and John had always known how to skin animals. They had learned a lot

51

about getting pelts ready for trade from the Delawares and French. But there were special skills for "best trade."

When Indians brought in poorer dressed skins, from otter, raccoon, skunk, panther, and deer, he and John would give them fifty cents to a dollar in credit. They would provide trade goods worth the amount of the money and sell the pelts for twice as much. So the Conner brothers would get about a dollar a skin to keep.

But "best skins"—excellent, rich beaver, fox and even bear—these could bring five to ten dollars apiece in Washington or New York if they were treated well. Could he bring in only "best skins" at his tiny post back home?

He could try. Mekinges could teach the skinners. William remembered the first time he had seen his wife dress pelts. He was amazed at the good job she did. First she made cuts around the animal's mouth and in the head. Then she pulled its body out through these openings, leaving the skin inside out. Then she thrust a strong hoop made of oak inside the skin and pulled that skin as tight as she could over it.

The secret was in the careful stretching, and in the way the underside was scraped. Every particle of fat or blood had to be removed or the fur was spoiled.

"Don't let the Indians leave fat on to raise the weight and get more money," John told his brother.

"I won't," William murmured.

"Or rocks in the skin. The tribal people know we pay for beaver skins by how much they weigh, and lately I have been finding stones and metal hidden beneath the skins," John said. Then he went on.

"Check the color of the skin side carefully. If it's yellow, you know it was killed at the right time of the year and will be full and rich. If it's blue, like some of the ones I've been finding, then the animal was killed at the wrong time of the year. It's a poor fur."

"I think we can get what you want." William was watching a young Delaware family outside the store. They had a small baby with them. They glanced around and spotted what they were looking for—the rain barrel on the porch.

Mekinges and John's wife stopped talking and watched the baby's mother through the open door. She took the top off the barrel. "What can she be doing?" William wondered.

The Delaware woman took the baby and plunged it into the cold water and held it under a moment.

William jumped from his stool, but Mekinges grabbed his sleeve. "Have you not seen that done? Well, perhaps not in a rain barrel. The baby is being toughened for the cold winters ahead. Do not go out there."

William sat back down and shook his head, but the baby seemed not to be the worse for wear. He was screaming for dear life, but then the mother hugged him and wrapped him up in warm furs.

The store was growing crowded with visitors. They were white men who had brought their families into the new treaty lands Harrison got from the Indians.

There were Indians, too, in the store. Everybody was drinking from the dipper at the whisky barrel. Two or three rough and scraggly trail scouts had made themselves comfortable on a bench by the door.

One of the Indians had been drinking too much. He was bragging to his friends. "I have killed more of these settlers than any warrior around," he said with slurred words.

"Down by The Trace I set fire to three cabins. I even took the scalp of a pretty, young white girl."

The white customers began to growl; they reached for their knives. Such talk made them hit the boiling point.

"Wait," one of the younger scouts said. He held up his hand, as if it say, "I'll handle this."

The Indian stumbled out of the store. Night had fallen, and John and William watched the young scout follow immediately.

"We'll never see that Indian again," William said and John nodded sadly. The peace they wanted, between two peoples they both cared about, had not come yet.

The next morning, after John's wife had fixed them all a big breakfast of hot biscuits and salt pork, William wandered outside the store.

"John's store is in a good location," he thought. It was right outside the Indian country and on the edge of the white population of the Whitewater Valley. The store could supply the stream of settlers coming into the valley and it was a place for people to meet each other and have a good time.

The men of the valley liked to get together here and play some of the games popular at the time. William looked through the early morning sun towards a group of settlers' sons. They were stringing up an old, live goose. They had stripped the feathers off the poor thing's neck and greased the neck till it was shiny.

"Keep holding that branch down," one boy said to another. "I've almost got this gander up!"

In a minute the boy let go, and the branch snapped back into the air. The goose was left flapping upside down with its feet firmly tied to a rope hanging from the branch.

William knew what they were doing. It was a gander-pull, done with a male goose. "Just like white men," he thought. Indians tried to be friends to all living things. If they had to kill an animal for food or fur, they apologized to his spirit. They never tried to hurt animals for fun, like these settlers were getting ready to do.

"I'll have a go first," one mean-looking boy said. He mounted his horse bareback quite a way back from the goose. Two men with switches in their hands whipped the horse on the behind. Off it went at a gallop.

The mean-looking boy reached out for the gander's greased neck as the horse raced by. His hand pulled hard on the greasy neck, making the poor gander's eyes bug out, but

54

he wasn't successful. You were supposed to pull the head off. That was the point of this bad game.

William watched the pitiful goose sputtering and flapping in the air, and thought it was a cruel game indeed.

"Look at that stranger," the men began to say to each other, pointing at William. "'Tis a strange crittur, ain't it? Be he Indian or white man or a little o' both?"

Then they began to laugh at William's Indian clothing and long, greased hair.

He decided to walk over to a shooting match that was going on behind the store. This game showed much more skill and made more sense than the stupid "gander pull" did. A man's rifle was like his best friend. It meant defense for his home and support for his family, because he used it to kill game for food almost every day.

The old scout stood at the bottom of a small hill preparing his rifle. "Come on, Alice, to the mark," he said to his gun. "I talk to Alice like she was a person," the scout said, winking at William. The gun did look special to William, a five-foot rifle with a slender polished grip and a silver plate on its side. The man was pouring powder from the clear, shiny horn of a cow into the palm of his hand.

William looked at the Kentucky rifle he had in his own hand. He carried it with him almost always, and though it didn't have a name, it served him well. He could hit a deer across any meadow you could name.

The old man was getting ready to shoot. "I don't like shootin' at the nail over thar on that tree as much as a target," he said. "What pillow-head went and chose nails anyways?

"Jest choose up your mark and quit complainin'," another said.

When the old man had poured enough powder to cover the bullet in his hand, he "tamped" it into the rifle and rammed the bullet home with a hickory ramrod.

He stood forty paces back from the tree with the nail in it and got ready to fire. William watched with a slight grin on his face. The others who were watching were trying to make the old man nervous, so he wouldn't shoot straight. One settler in particular kept clicking his tongue in and out, making it sound like a horse galloping.

The old man knew he had three tries to hit the nail. If he missed after three tries, he would be out. He planted his feet with his left side towards the nail. "Click, click, click," went the man's clicking tongue behind him. The old man raised Alice, his rifle, took aim and fired her.

He missed. Second try, he missed again. On the third try his neck veins were sticking out and sweat came down his forehead.

Just as he fired the gun there was another loud "click."

As the bullet missed the nail for the last time, the old scout threw down the rifle. "He threw me off, dad-blame it. Ol' Jim Brewer, I'll make a target out o' you!" He ran off into the woods after his tormentor.

Others were taking out powder horns, loading their own rifles. Some of the best men in the Whitewater Valley waited to take their turns, but that morning no one could hit the nail more than twice. No one, that is until William Conner came to the line. Once, twice, three times he made the nail ring out. The scout, returning from his chase and watching William shoot, said, "Looks like an Injeean, but shoots like a ranger. Who is he anyways?"

"Will Conner. White Indian, so they say. "But who cares if he's Tom Q. Jefferson efn he can shoot like that." Then they left to go to the store to get another drink from the whisky barrel.

Chapter Six
Troubles with Tecumseh

The fur-trading business John and William Conner had set up grew through the next seven years. But so did the troubles in Indiana. Settlers were pouring into the Territory, and into many areas of the Old Northwest, forcing the Indians to give up more and more land.

In the year 1810 Governor William Henry Harrison called John Conner to meet with him in Vincennes, at Grouseland, his beautiful home near the Wabash River.

"You grew up among Indians, John. It is well known that the Delawares like and respect you," Harrison said, as he stirred a cup of tea in the parlor. "That's why I have called on you in the last few years to serve as an interpreter of what Indians say at the treaties."

Harrison went on. "You know that both Presidents Jefferson and Madison wanted the Indians and whites to be able to live together in peace in this new part of the country. They tried to get them to farm, but the Indians just haven't been able to catch on."

"I understand that, sir, but where do I fit in?" John asked.

"Ever since the last treaty, the Treaty of Ft. Wayne, the Indians have been unhappy," Harrison answered.

"They lost several million acres in that one treaty," John Conner pointed out.

"Yes. So far they have had no one to be their voice, but now a voice has arisen. Te-cum-seh, the Shawnee, and his brother, The Prophet, are stirring the Indians up. 'Do not give up any more land. We must draw the line,' is what they are riding around saying."

"I knew who Tecumseh was when he lived on White River," John said. "He's a smart man with a fearsome anger. Still, the Delawares don't want war, I can tell you that."

"I need you to go down to the Delaware towns. The Prophet and Tecumseh are Shawnee Indians, but they are visiting the Delawares to get them to join them in making war on us. John, see what the Prophet and Tecumseh are doing. If the Delawares do want peace, maybe they can get Tecumseh to give up his ideas."

John put his teacup on the table and stood up.

"And another thing," Harrison said, also getting out of his chair. "See if you can find any stolen horses. We've had scores disappear from the Territory."

60

John arrived at the peaceful White River towns to find them anything but peaceful. Tecumseh had stirred up the pot of trouble and made it boil. John Conner sat in the shadows, unseen, as the great War Chief Tecumseh spoke to Chief Anderson.

"We must not let the whites take any more of our land!" Tecumseh said, his voice loud and firm. "This William Henry Harrison tricked us when he made us sign the papers. All Indians own the land together.

"No single tribe can sell the land. Harrison knew this. We must fight for what is ours! Brother, will you join us?" He leaned towards Chief Anderson.

Anderson answered him calmly. "No, Tecumseh. The Delawares will not fight against Americans. We have been too close to each other. Besides, the Great White Owl of my boyhood dream has spoken again. He came to me in a vision last night. He said, 'Do not fight the white man. Do not accept his ways, but do not fight either. The white men are impossible to stop. They have the power.'

"I made a promise to the Great Owl that I would always obey him when he spoke. I will not disobey." John Conner, in his place, out of sight, felt Chief Anderson's eyes on him. Should he come forward? Now might be a good time to tell Tecumseh General Harrison's important message. He got up and went to the campfire.

He bowed to the Shawnee chief. "Tecumseh," he said in the Shawnee tongue he knew so well, "You are a strong and important Shawnee. My mother was raised by the Shawnees, and your relatives are known to her as wise men. Surely your wisdom will let you see the folly of a revolt against the Americans.

"All the Indian tribes together cannot defeat the guns of the white man. Besides, the white man never has been good at telling Indian tribes apart. Innocent ones, like the Delawares, could be hurt. Do not do this thing."

61

Tecumseh stood tall and looked directly at John Conner. "You, white Indian, as they call you, I say you mock those who were your blood brothers. You pretend to be the tribal peoples' friend, but you help the whites take the land in the treaties. You are a man of two faces, and I scorn you. I go to Prophetstown."

He turned on his heel, ordering the tribal men with him to prepare to leave. His destination was the Indian village his brother was forming, where the Tipp-e-canoe meets the Wabash. Here, at least, were men who would listen to him.

John Conner was stunned. Tecumseh had said, "Those who were your blood brothers—." How could Tecumseh have known about Running Wolf and the sacred pledge they had all made so many years ago?

The answer was behind him, in the shadows.

"John Conner, it is I, Running Wolf." John turned joyfully, but the Delaware's hard, cold face made him stop in his tracks.

"Blood brothers we may be, but not friends," Running Wolf said. The eyes of the Indian were grim. He did not offer his arm for the arm slap greeting.

"I told you I would not stand for too much change in tribal ways. When it comes to taking our land, too much is too much. Even my own people do not understand. Most of these Delawares are old women. All they talk about is peace and friendship with Americans." He looked with scorn at Chief Anderson.

"And you are not for peace and friendship?" John asked.

"I am not. Nor am I an old woman. I follow Tecumseh."

"I am sorry to hear it. There will be much pain for tribesmen and whites alike."

"And who will you ride with? You who were loved by the Delawares and married one of ours. What of William Conner? You are both sworn blood brothers, and husbands to women of the tribes. You of all else should understand what

62

is being done to our tribal peoples. Will you stand by and let us all be destroyed?"

John Conner was silent. He did not know what to say.

"Well," said Running Wolf bitterly, "we all must choose. And each must be true to what he is. Your skin is burnt by sun and wind. It is as brown as dirt, as dark as a Delaware's. But under the brown skin is white blood."

"Running Wolf—" said John. Through his mind rushed the images of the easy days when they were young in Ohio, hunting the woods, playing their games.

When Running Wolf answered, his voice was softer. "I do not blame you, John Conner, no, nor William either. A catbird may sing on a branch. He may sing and sing and tell the world and even himself that he is a warbler, but catbird he does remain. It is Nature's way."

John decided to follow Tecumseh's party. He knew it would be the most dangerous journey of his life. If Tecumseh should find him, not even his blood-brother Running Wolf could save him. And John was not sure his old friend would want to, now.

Harrison had told him, though, to keep an eye on Tecumseh and his brother. John let Tecumseh get an hour ahead of him and then he set out, walking down the trail. He didn't want Tecumseh to know he was being followed.

Walking the path he knew so well, John noticed the trail of Tecumseh and his tribesmen went off down a smaller and less used way. John's sharp eyes picked out little signs that showed the Indians had been this way. A broken branch, trampled grass, and a few brown leaves wet side up all showed men had walked through here. John knew trouble was brewing because the tribesmen had been sloppy about covering their trail.

John quickened his steps, trying to catch up with Tecumseh. The crisp, fall air bit into his lungs as he trotted along the moonlit path. He smelled the smoke of a burning campfire drifting across the cool night air. He knew he must be getting close.

"I wondered why they are travelling on foot. They probably are going to take horses. This may even be heading for the camp where they are hiding all the territory's stolen horses," John thought as he crept close to Tecumseh's camp. The Indians were busy roasting rabbit on a spit over the fire. John glanced around their camp, but he saw no signs of horses yet.

Tecumseh finished eating his rabbit. He went off by himself, leaving the others to their work. He was an intelligent, careful man who would not take an active part in a war party. But he did not mind if other tribesmen caused the whites to fear, if it served the cause of the Indians.

Running Wolf was in charge of the raid that was to come. He gestured to the men about him. Running Wolf and the rest stood and began putting a mixture of charcoal and bear oil on their faces. They drew black lines.

As soon as the group was prepared, with guns and tomahawks ready, Running Wolf led them to the path. Standing tall and proud in the moonlight, he let out a loud scalp yell. John crept closer, ready to follow him. Running Wolf lit a hickory torch and left camp.

Creeping behind as closely as he dared, John followed Running Wolf down the dark path without making a sound. After all, Running Wolf had taught him all he knew!

He could see smoke floating out of a distant chimney. Surely Running Wolf would not order his men to kill tonight! That would risk too much. Harrison would bring an army to kill them all.

No, he wished to scare the pioneers. That was it. Scare them so they would not think it was so easy to take land from the tribes.

Running Wolf stood on the edge of a tall field of corn that was ready for fall harvest. He raised his hand, then let it fall,

grimly. The giant stalks of corn crackled as the men lit the edge of the field on fire.

Running Wolf let out an ear-piercing yelp and the other five tribesmen followed. A scream sounded from inside the distant cabin. Instantly it was muffled by someone's hand.

The flames quickly scorched a wide path across the field, and the warriors went boldly near the cabin, yelling their scalp yells.

Then they went to the horse pen and let out the horses and mounted them, bareback. They brought one for Tecumseh. John stood behind a tree as the group dashed by. They would take the horses to Prophetstown, he was sure. That was where all the stolen horses in the territory must be.

Harrison was right, John told himself. Tecumseh was getting ready for war. All of the Northwest could become a battle ground. Indians and whites could go on killing each other for years. Quickly he retraced his path to the Dela-

The Battle of Tippecanoe

ware camp to get himself a horse. He must return and report to Harrison. Tecumseh had to be stopped, and soon.

That "soon" time came, in November of 1811, when Tecumseh left his brother The Prophet and went into the South to try to get tribes there to join with him. Harrison chose this time to take an army to Prophetstown. He called on John Conner to be part of a scout group at the front of the army.

Governor Harrison hoped not to have to fight the tribes. He hoped they would break up the camp. He sent the peaceful Delawares to Prophetstown to take word that they must leave the war camp, that there must be peace. William Conner was with the messenger Delawares. The Prophet and other Indians there made fun of the Delawares and told them to go away.

Many tribal peoples in the Prophetstown camp did not want peace. Harrison's army camped near the Tippecanoe River with 1,000 men. They were not far from the huge Indian camp at Prophetstown, where hundreds of Winn-e-be-gos, Shawnees, Sauk Fox, Kick-a-poo, Pot-a-wa-to-mi and Miamis lived.

Part of the U.S. army was in Harrison's camp. There were also settlers in militia units from Indiana and Kentucky. John Conner was with them. Everyone talked of battle as they slept near their guns around the campfires. John Conner was with the scout group, and he slept with his gun and powder horn next to him.

Running Wolf had told him, "You will have to choose." He had made his choice. He would fight against the Indians. It seemed natural to him to do this. After all, he was white. "A catbird is a catbird, no matter how much he pretends he is some other bird," was a true saying.

It was the morning of November 7, 1811. As the troops slept, before dawn, the Indians surrounded them.

The Battle of Tippecanoe was fast and furious. After two hours of fighting, the Americans managed to drive the tribal men back and chased them all away, killing many. Over two hundred Americans were killed or wounded, too. John Conner was not hurt in the Battle of Tippecanoe.

The settler army burned Prophetstown. When Tecumseh came back, he decided to go to Canada and join the British. The British were just starting to fight the Americans in the War of 1812. The British used the Indians to help them fight the Americans.

Soon both William and John Conner found themselves part of the Indian Wars. John was a scout for Harrison. He rode throughout Indiana Territory, keeping an eye on the tribes, and then let Harrison know if any of the Indians were planning raids or war.

William, still living as a white Indian, was very troubled about the war. He was the father of three half-Indian, half-white children now, John, James, and William, and he did not wish to fight Indians. He cared about them and he was married to one!

Indian raiding parties, pushed into action by the British, had worked their way into much of Indiana. They even threatened Ft. Harrison and beseiged Ft. Wayne. There were a few killings. Indiana was a place of brutal fighting and fear.

Most of the Delawares did not wish to fight, and William was with them in spirit, as always. A small number of Delawares did join Tecumseh, and William wondered if Running Wolf was among the "Fighting Delawares." William worked to end the war quickly, so all might live in peace again. During this time, though, the Americans burned some Delaware villages on White River to the ground. When William heard of it, it made him sad. He knew John, wherever he was in this war, would be sad, too.

One day in 1812, William leaned his forehead against the warm mantel of his fireplace and thought about the troubles. Word had come that at Pigeon Roost twenty-four men, women and children had all been killed by an Indian war party.

William thought, "Pigeon Roost! What a coincidence. How long ago it was that John and I were afraid of the pigeons. Rebecca told us not to be afraid of change."

How things had changed! Indiana was in a state of war, and 2,000 volunteers from Kentucky were helping fight off the Indians in the territory.

William was in charge of a little group of loyal Indians. "We have been ridin' around trying to try to stop the British Indians from hurting settlers in Indiana and Ohio. I think we have been doin' some good," he told his wife. "How I wish we were back in the simpler times, when we could hunt, fish, and work at the trading post."

"Will you be leaving soon?" Mekinges asked. She was picking nettles off her son's leggings. "You have just come. We miss you so much." Their sons John and James played with corn cobs on the floor of the cabin.

The Battle of the Thames

William answered her, "Harrison has called me to help scout a party goin' to find the Miamis along the Miss-iss-in-e-wa River south of us here. We must keep them from goin' over to the British. And then—we must go to Canada. Harrison is tryin' to get Lake Erie under American control. The whole army must go to Canada. That is where the British headquarters is. Tecumseh is goin' north with his Indians. We must destroy them, or there will never be peace here, for our Delawares, or anybody else."

"And so you leave in the morning," his wife said sadly.

"And so I leave in the morning," he answered.

William shivered on a cold October day in Canada at what is called The Battle of The Thames. He was part of the group in charge of grabbing the enemy cannons at the right time.

As he waited with the 2,500 men of the American army, a scout came in. "They have an equal amount of British and

69

Indians," the scout said, panting. " 'Twill not be an easy battle."

So much depended on this fight. Peace in Indiana for both white and Indian, nothing else. "Well," William thought, "we have somethin' the British don't. We have the wild Kentucky cavalry." Everybody knew about them. They were big, tough men who galloped about doing what they wanted to, but they could be fine fighters.

The battle began. The troopers, riding huge, strong horses, rode straight for the enemy battle line. They shot to the left and right with a mad fury, dropping British soldiers like flies. Another squadron of cavalry rushed through the underbrush to the left, sending hiding Indians running for their lives.

William tried to keep up with all the action, but he did not even get to grab the cannons. The action was over soon, because of one very important shot.

It was the shot that killed Tecumseh, War Chief of the tribesmen. He fell, the Indians fled, and the battle was finished.

"Conner, come over here," someone called out. William stepped over the corpses scattered around the ground to a group of American soldiers. They were huddled over something.

"Let's see what he says," one militiaman said, looking up at William. "Well, did we or did we not bag the big one?"

The militiamen stepped back, revealing the limp and bloody body of what they thought was Tecumseh. William nodded that he thought so, although he couldn't be completely sure, because the body had been cut up by the soldiers. He couldn't help but feel a little sad. Tecumseh had been his neighbor for six years on the White River, in a time when there was peace.

He turned his back on the body. One of the militiamen had begun to cut long strips of skin from Tecumseh's thighs to make into razor straps! "And they say the Indians are savages," thought William.

As he turned, he saw something from the corner of his eye. It was a limp arm dangling over a log. On the arm was a bright wolf tattoo, like the fading one on his own arm. William slowly crept across the grass. He was afraid of what he might find.

He stooped and turned the fallen Indian over. A sense of shock and sadness filled him. There, relaxed and peaceful looking, lay Running Wolf. He had died fighting with Tecumseh.

If Running Wolf, and Tecumseh too, had only listened to Chief Anderson, they might be alive today. All this trouble might not have happened.

"The white men are impossible to stop. They have the power."

That was what Chief Anderson had said.

It was true. There was no use fighting useless fights. Now a great leader was dead and hundreds of Indians and white men with him.

William looked across the bloody battlefield. There were dead bodies heaped in all directions. Indians and whites had fallen across each other.

William thought again of Rebecca the Indian woman. "Rebecca looked for changes, and now these changes have caused her son to die," he said to himself sadly.

He turned south, heading for home. As he rode, he wondered something. Who was worse? The white men for taking land and bringing death? Or the Indians for not facing the truth when it stared them in the face and giving up peacefully?

Or was it he, himself, William Conner, who still felt like a white Indian and was torn between them both.

Chapter Seven

The Great Migration

Before the War of 1812 even ended, John Conner stood on the threshold of his trading post in the Whitewater valley watching the latest group of pioneers pass by. A wagon piled high with all kinds of baggage swayed as its laboring ox pulled the heavy load. Six small, dirty faces peered out of a canvas cover. The father of the family drove a small herd of cattle behind the oxen wagon, while the mother tried to drive the ox on in front.

"People are beginning to come already," thought John. "Soon there will be thousands. Everyone believes the Indians will be defeated in the War of 1812. People were only waiting back east for that news, and now they are swarming into the Northwest. Times are changing for America."

Times were also continuing to change for the Conners. John Conner's Indian wife had died. He was sad, but also glad she did not have to see the defeated, bitter people of all tribes return to burnt-out homes as the war ended.

The Delawares would have to move on again. They wanted to stay in Indiana, but the government wanted them to go on the road to new homes in the West. The white man was pushing them out.

John sighed and looked around him. His trading post had grown. His land was now a 320-acre farm. More settlers were moving in next to him and the woods were disappearing.

He watched his lovely young neighbor, Lavina Winship, swing down off her horse and come into the trading post store. "Maybe it's time to think about a new wife in these new times," he thought.

Soon John Conner began calling at the Winship cabin. Finally he asked Jabez Winship, his old friend and neighbor, for Lavina's hand in marriage. John and Lavina were married March 13, 1813.

John was proud to bring Lavina home to see the growing little town they were calling Connersville. He had laid out town lots along the river bank, and already people had built log cabins.

"This is a palace, John," Lavina said, smiling. " 'Tisn't really a cabin at all. It has a wood floor, not dirt. The chimney is made of stone, not clay. And just look at that nice rope feather bed. 'Tisn't goin' to be any trouble keepin' house here."

"Really, I hope you aren't just sayin' that Lavina. Your pa thinks I'm a backwoodsman, but I'm not. When I build you a new wood house, he'll change his mind."

She busied herself by the fire cooking. In an hour she was unmolding pound cakes. She had baked them in coffee cups, and when she put them on a plate, they looked like huge snowballs with icing dripping off. "When the berries are ripe, I'll bake the likes of something you've never seen, John," she said.

John shook his head in wonder at how different his life had become.

Three years passed, and John Conner's farming and store-keeping were making him rich.

On a particularly bright day in 1816, he pulled a chair up to the breakfast table. His father-in-law Jabez Winship had been spending the night at the cabin. "Well, Jabez," John said. "Today I leave for Corydon. I wonder what it will be like now that I'm a member of the legislative Assembly for the new State of Indiana."

It sounded odd to say "state." Indiana, under its first governor, Jonathan Jennings, had just been admitted to the Union. It had set up a state constitution.

"I have to say that I'm s'prised, too," the old settler said. "Never thought you two white Indians would turn out to be worth much. But—what will you senators be doing in the state capital, son-in-law?"

"Gettin' the things in the Constitution movin'. We say we'll provide for public education, prisons, asylums for the old and sick. But what we really must handle this time is land. That's what people really care about."

The legislature was going to set up new counties, straighten out the boundary lines of old ones and decide on the county seats where courts would be held.

Lavina poured boiling water over a toasted corn dodger loaded with maple syrup and handed a steaming cupful of "mush" to her father, and he nodded his thanks.

"I don't envy you all the travelin'," Jabez Winship said.

"Oh, I won't have trouble travellin' down to Corydon," John said. "I can use the Whitewater Trail most of the way to the Ohio River. Let's hope these butterflies in my belly disappear by the time I reach the capital building."

His father-in-law stared at John's collar and shirt. "You're all dressed up like a pig gone to market," he said.

"Well, maybe not a pig. But it is amazin'," John answered. "John Conner, the old trapper and scout, raised among the Indians, is a State Senator," He smiled and winked at his father-in-law, and helped himself to a corn dodger and molasses.

Butterflies and all, John arrived at the capital, Corydon, for the first meeting of the state's General Assembly. "Ah, 'tis not as fancy as I had heard," he said.

The town had less than one hundred buildings, most of them log cabins of different sizes. John walked around an occasional stump and avoided garbage in the streets. Two hogs snorted their way past, heading for the good things in a nearby garden.

The capitol building stood out among the trees in the distance. It was a simple, but beautiful two story structure made of stone. At its top was a little steeple with a small bell in it.

John got down from his horse. Kicking at some scraggly puppies who had come out of a barnyard to play and nip at his ankles, he opened the door.

He looked around at the large open room downstairs and saw stairs leading to two more rooms upstairs. The smells of tobacco, sweat, and drying wool floated out. John Tipton, his old friend in the fur trade, waved to him from across the room.

"Welcome, Conner," Tipton said, shaking John's hand. "Good to see you, my friend." He turned his head and spat tobacco juice on the floor.

"My friend Senator Beggs has got his dander up," Tipton said. "Some of the backwoods senators are callin' him 'Mr. Grammar' 'cause he always talks so fancy, and he's hoppin' mad."

John smiled at this. He knew that Hoosiers liked their politicians to be simple men. They frowned on those they thought too "high falootin.' " In those days the senators put their feet up on desks and shouted at things they didn't like. John thought he ought to fit in pretty well.

Chairs creaked and the first meeting began.

In the next few years John Conner helped pass bills to organize many things in the new state. He helped create a new county, Fayette, where his trading post was located.

The young state was growing. But the truth was that the Indians still occupied two thirds of the state. Soon the senators wanted to try to get the Indians to give up more of their land.

John Conner thought about it for a while and then decided to support the treaty. Time doesn't stand still, after all.

And you'd better learn to move with it too, he thought, or you'll be left in the dust while the cart goes on down the road without you.

"It's easy for you to say, 'Get the Delawares to sign this treaty,'" William said one afternoon to John. "You sit there in your new frame house next to your new sawmill, with your white wife and white son. What about all our Indian friends? What will the future be for them? Don't you care?"

"I do care, William," John said, stretching his long legs out. "It's just that if Indiana is to be a real state, well, the truth is, the Indians probably have to go. There are too many white people who want this land. The lands west of the Mississippi River are fertile and full of game. You know our friends'll be happier there."

William sulked by the fire. He didn't always understand John. It seemed to him they were betraying their friends. Was what he said true? Would the Indians be better off in the West? He did not know, but he did know that both he and John would have to help with the new treaty, which was going to be signed at St. Mary's, in western Ohio. The cub Running Wolf had tattooed on his arm ached a lot lately, almost as much as his heart did.

Two months later, St. Mary's, usually a tiny settlement, swarmed with people. Families, treaty officials, traders and Indians all camped out waiting for the treaty to be signed.

William Conner strode about, watching the scene. It seemed to him more like a carnival than anything else. "These settlers have come to see the Indians sign away the lands they love and live on," he thought. "They think of it like a travelling show."

He listened to the settlers talking. "They should get out," one said.

"Only good Indian is a dead Indian," another answered.

The settlers wanted the farmlands. They also needed new roads built over the Indians' land so they could ship their products to markets.

This was really what the treaty was about.

"This is an overnight town," William told John as they walked about St. Mary's. The river bank bulged with Indian huts and tents. Cabins were quickly put up to serve as boarding houses for the treaty signers. Army barracks had gone up overnight. There were troops to be sure nothing got out of hand.

"Some of these trade goods aren't good quality," John said to William as they investigated the traders' displays. The tribal people and their wives did not seem to care. They crowded around the pots and pans, skirts and caps.

"It's been a long time since I've seen so many Indians together," said William. "Potawatomis, Weas, Delawares, Miamis are all here—all called to sign the treaty. You don't usually see 'em 'round the same campfire."

"And the Wyandots, Senecas, Shawnees and Ot-ta-was have come to see the other tribes sign."

"If, indeed, they all do sign this treaty."

78

Games and activities were going on all around the Conners. "I'm a better man than you are," one man was shouting from across the tables.

"Oh, yeah, we see about that," an Indian answered him. And the "rasslin' match" was on.

The two burly men stripped off their shirts and put their fists up. White and Indian men formed a circle about them.

"Throw him a good one." "Go for the eyes," people shouted.

The white man aimed for his opponent's eyes. He had long finger nails that were as tough and sharp as horns. But the Indian ducked and socked him on the chin.

Punches flew. Then the two men started throwing each other about.

The Indian bit the white man's shoulder and then held him to the ground for the count of ten, thus ending the fight.

The crowd broke up, and the treaty talks began.

John and William Conner walked back to the council ring. William said, "Some folk say you and I have the power to either get the tribesmen to sign this treaty or not. We are the friends of the Indians. We are the go-betweens."

"Whether we tell them to or not, the government is going to get the land. Better now, and in peace than with trouble later, I have decided," John said.

"I s'pose you're right," William said. I can hardly stomach it. But it may be best. The best of two bad choices."

"The Weas, Potawatomis and Delawares have signed," said John later to William, "Now all that is needed is Chief Richardville of the Miamis."

"I'll try to talk to him," William said.

"One thing more, brother," John said. "It is about your land. It is on the acres the Delawares will be leaving because of this treaty. You had better get someone to promise you that land, or all your work through these years'll be lost."

William asked Governor Jonathan Jennings to be sure he was given the land he had lived on. "Do not worry about it.

I'll see that it's yours," Jennings said. But he did not keep his promise.

On October 3, 1818, the Treaty of St. Mary's was signed. As a part of it, the U.S. government agreed to supply the Delawares with 120 horses, proper food and clothing and $4,000 in silver coins each year. They had three years to leave their lands along the White River.

William travelled back to Connersville with John before going home. He was not happy. Things were changing fast—too fast for him.

Not only would his friends, the Delawares, be leaving, but there was much more to worry about. There was a good chance that Mekinges and his children, now six in number, would go with them.

It was strong custom among the Indians that a woman stay with her people, and the children with their mother if parents separated. He did not know if he could stand it if they left.

"At least I have my land," he told himself. It wasn't an Indian thought. It was a white thought. The tribes thought all land belonged to everybody.

William Conner spurred his horse. Whatever the future held, he was eager to get home.

Chapter Eight
Horseshoe Prairie

William thought a lot about being lonely these days. He always had his family for company and the Indians for friends. Somehow knowing the Delawares would be leaving soon made him feel empty inside.

But something new was happening, too. He would never really be alone again, even after the Delawares left. A warm spring breeze gently brushed his cheeks as he watched a group of new settlers arrive to settle near him, on what was now being called Horseshoe Prairie.

The settlers were from Connersville, from near where his brother John lived. He had sent them to settle on this land, now that the Treaty of St. Mary's had made it possible for white people to come in.

These new pioneers were the Finches, the Shirtses, the Lacys, the Bushes, and the Willisons. William went over to lug heavy logs and move brush aside so the men could build log cabins for their families.

William liked lending a hand; it was necessary in such a harsh, raw, wilderness. It made him feel important, needed. Then, too, he was glad there would be friends near his own home.

The spring after they had settled in on the prairie, the families planted crops on the fertile land. William helped them girdle trees, cutting rings all around the trunks. The

81

trees would die, then, and the settlers could pull the stumps out and farm the fields.

One day in June, William visited Horseshoe Prairie to see the new corn shoots between the dying trees. Solomon Finch and his son George were lighting a green, wood-smoke fire. They hoped the smoke would keep the millions of mosquitoes away while they milked their cows. "I never thought I'd see the day Connersville would seem like a paradise, but town livin' sure beats this wilderness," young George said.

The thick smoke helped to keep down the flies, but William could still hear the high-pitched hum of mosquitoes as he watched George milk the cows.

Tiny drops of blood began to drip off the boy's arms where the bugs bit him as he milked. George dabbed the drops off his arms and looked through the cow's swishing tail at his father.

Solomon was sitting by the fire, very ill with fever, or malarial ague. His teeth chattered as chills shook his body.

"Another fit comin' on. Get on back to the cabin. I'll be up by and by," he said.

"Solomon, we have to get you some quinine," said William. How long have you been havin' the fits?"

"Weeks, seems like," the older man said. "I shake and chill and get weak. Then I take to bed for a week or so. Finally the sweats come and I feel better."

"Take care of yourself. I don't want to bury anyone else on Horseshoe Prairie." Last Saturday Mr. Shirts' wife had died.

William had never had much trouble with ague and other sicknesses. Maybe it was because he had lived with Indians for so long. But these city folk seemed weak. It was hard when no doctors were near, and no apothecaries. He sometimes sent Indian medicine over, elm bark in water, or wild cherry cordial. But if many other people got sick this summer he and Mekinges would not have enough time to take care of them all.

William stayed at the Finch cabin that night. About midnight George Finch sat upright in bed. Outside, wolves were howling. The cows would be in danger. He needed to go check them.

"Be careful, George," Mr. Finch said weakly from the corner.

"Do you want me to help you?" William asked.

"No. Have to learn to be a pioneer myself," George mumbled.

William watched from the hole that was the window. George was heading towards the cow pen. Two red eyes dared him to come any closer. George put the pine chip lantern down, loaded his gun, and fired it toward the red eyes.

A wolf slunk into the darkness. George raised the lantern to the cows in the pen. One had a hole in its throat.

The next morning William looked at the wounded cow. He put a white walnut poultice over the deep gash. Solomon Finch called him back to the cabin. "George looks sick. He's starting the shakes, William," he said.

Soon William was by the young man's side. George's father said, "When I started in with the ague, I hung a spider round my neck and took calomel." Calomel was a bitter medicine people took for the ague. "Don't you think we should give him some of that?"

"No. But Peru bark, quinine, would help, if we had any." The settlement was out of quinine. So many were ill. William returned to his own lands. In two more days he visited the Finches again.

He looked in the small back room to see George shaking and moaning. He looked very ill. "Galloping ague," William said, shaking his head.

"Will he get well?" Mr. Finch asked. His voice sounded worried.

"Only time will tell. Give him the herb tea I left for you. But in these wetlands—well, a lot of folk stay sick here most every summer. Seems like folk in every cabin are sick now. I have to go take some corn to your brother."

Elizabeth Chapman watched gratefully as William unloaded corn from his wagon. Her stepfather, John Finch, usually had something to barter for the corn, but not this time.

"We are beholden to you. You do not have to share in these hard times," she said.

"I learned Indian ways long ago. Whatever one person owns, is really owned by all. Running Wolf, my friend—"

But he did not go on. Thinking of his friend made him sad.

The cold frosts of fall finally seemed to kill off the worst of the ague, but not before George Finch died. For the rest of the settlement, though, life became more normal.

A big event came in May of 1820. The State Assembly sent ten men to pick out a new place for a state capital.

Lots of the good sites were around William's property. The group had been told to meet at his house, and the news that important men, Governor Jennings and General John Tipton, would be near Horseshoe Prairie made the settlers buzz with excitement.

The men came. William was glad he would see his brother, for John was one of the commissioners. William pumped John's arm up and down in a hefty handshake when he came in, and they both greeted the other nine men who soon rode up.

Standing under the huge sycamore tree outside William's double log cabin, the Governor and his men talked about their plans. "Let's divide up. Ludlow, you and Gililand go up to the spot where Fall Creek and White River meet. John will lead the way. Tipton and I will go look at the hills over the river up yonder. William, will you lead the way for us?"

So the two groups set out to look for a new capital city for the State of Indiana.

84

The group William led were in no hurry. Governor Jennings said he loved a chance to relax in the out-of-doors.

The horses walked single file along the high bluffs above White River as the May sun kept everyone pleasantly warm.

Governor Jennings reined his horse. "Let's get a better view of that river," he said. White River rolled lazily along as far as the eye could see. Fifty feet below the trail, the glassy water shone in the sun.

"Would you look at that sight? I'm amazed. I've never seen so many fish in one spot," the governor said. The smooth water seemed to be wearing a blanket of fish.

Monster-size muskelunge, the hated gar fish, and just about every other fish in the world looked like they had gathered to sleep in the sun.

"Let's take a break and try our luck," Governor Jennings cried.

William was more than happy to obey. He was surprised when Jennings untied a long fishing spear called a "gig" from the back of his saddle. "He's not all politics, I see," William thought.

Governor Jennings and the other men in the party spent the rest of the afternoon fishing the teeming waters of White River. Soon, though, they had to return to business: finding a capital city for the state of Indiana. They mounted their horses and rode off.

The other group of men had surveyed a spot thirteen miles south of William's house, where Fall Creek flowed into the White River. Finally the men all decided that the Fall Creek spot would be the best capital. The new city was dubbed "Indiana-polis" which meant, city of Indiana.

Governor Jennings told William, "This new city is going to make a real difference in this part of the state, and in your land, William. More people will be coming to settle, and the city will buy produce from your farm. You can send your grain and hogs to market. Your life is going to change."

After the men left, as William thought about their visit, he felt proud they had chosen his house as a meeting place. It seemed that he and John were getting to be important people in Indiana, more important than they ever thought they would be.

"Mekinges served their meals so nicely," he thought looking at the wife he had loved so many years. His six children were growing to be strong boys and girls. He loved them too.

"But I did wish I had a bigger house for the visitors. They couldn't all sleep in my cabin."

He sat down on his bed and ran his hands over the leather straps of the well-worn trunk resting on the floor. "I've never really used all this money," he thought, digging his hands into a huge pile of silver dollars. Years of fur trading had made William a rich man.

Mekinges was sweeping the floor. "Soon her people will leave," he thought. "It is right, I know it. These are hunting people. They hate farming. They have no life at all here and no dignity. People look down on them. Maybe out West they can get back their dignity."

He looked up at his wife. "And will you stay with me?" he wondered. He had been afraid to ask her before.

She came to him. Her eyes were sad. "You know it is the custom that Delaware women stay with the tribe. And the children with the mother."

William's heart ached 'till he thought it would break. "I know." He had been afraid for so long that she would say it.

"And, husband, I know you will not go with me, though we care for each other. We each must be what we must be. I told you before you married me that a white Indian is not an Indian."

"Yes, and the truth is I am NOT an Indian, though I have loved their life so much. And from now on I am going to have to live like a white. This new village and now the new capital are creeping up all about me. I have to stay, and I have to live white now. But I wish you would change your mind and stay with me. You could learn some of these new things."

"I do not think so. It was one thing when we lived as Indians, quite another if we must live as whites. Think of me, William Conner. I must live free. I cannot make quilts and embroider sayings from the Bible as these white women do."

And so, one sad day, Mekinges and the children mounted horses and went west with their tribe. William had provided well for all of them with plenty of money and ponies. Sadly he said goodbye.

We must choose, Running Wolf had said. Yes, it is true, we all must choose, William thought as he walked back to the loneliness of his empty cabin. Life in these woods was hard, very hard. But it would not work at all if you pretended to be something you were not. Running Wolf had been right, William thought. Still, that did not make William feel any better.

A short while later William's small house was crowded with men. Pipe smoke twirled in blue streaks above his head. He squinted through the pale candle light across the wooden table. A group of Horseshoe Prairie men had gathered for an evening of card playing and gambling.

William gathered up his latest winnings and thought of the days he had played moccasin and cherry stone with the Delawares. Now it was whist, with these pioneer men who had become his friends. Then an idea came to him.

"I've always been a good gambler. Maybe I can take my winnings from the old life I led and bet them on a new one. It's sure I can't make money by trading with the Indians I knew. Most of them are gone. But I do have something most whites want—lots of land. If I play my cards right I can sell land and pick up some winnings in the white man's world. Perhaps I can buy myself a future."

William laid his hand of cards on the table. "That's what I'll do," he thought. "I'll not be afraid to change. I also better think about another wife. My first one is not coming back, and the truth is, I am very lonely. I can't have men in my cabin playing cards every minute of the time to keep me company."

It was hard for William to adjust to his new life, and missing Mekinges didn't help matters. But without her it was also easier to live the life of a white man in these changing times. Three months after the departure of Mekinges and his children, William asked for the hand of seventeen-year-old Elizabeth Chapman.

William knew that Elizabeth came from a totally different background. She had lived an easy life in New York with her mother and brother. She never had any contact with Indians, and had no experience living out in the wild frontier town until she came to Horseshoe Prairie. William was going to have to change a lot to live with her!

William had seen that she was a brave and strong young woman when she had helped him nurse the sick of the settlement in the time of ague. She was just the sort of woman William knew he needed to succeed in the days to come.

Although it was November 30, it turned into a warm Indian summer day for the wedding of William and Elizabeth. All the settlers in the area were there on the grounds of John Finch's cabin for the ceremony. The men were dressed in buckskin trousers and vests, the women in homespun blue or brown dresses. They all were waiting for a wedding to begin.

William Conner, tall and sure of himself, stood in the wooden doorway. He thought of his other wedding day. Mekinges had been beautiful with a silk-ribboned skirt and a crown of flowers on her head. "Don't think of the past," he told himself. "It isn't easy to forget. Still, I must."

Smiling, he took his shy, slim bride by the hand. Fielding Hazelrigg, a justice of the peace from Connersville, began the ceremony.

Out of the corner of his eye, William could see some old Indian friends from the Miami tribe who had come to watch the wedding. He wondered what they thought of this white man's ceremony. Here there was no gifting of presents to the bride's parents, no simple "Let us live together now."

As the ceremony continued, he saw the Indians pull back to the edge of the woods. He slipped a ring on Elizabeth's finger. The people around him bowed their heads and prayed the Lord's Prayer. When he turned, the Indians had gone from the clearing.

John stepped up to William and solemnly shook his hand. "Congratulations, brother. May you be as happy as I have been." His wife Lavina smiled too, and led them to the tables. The usual backwoods wedding feast was about to begin.

Although the tables were wooden boards set on saw horses, they shone with china, pewter, and linen. The women of the settlement had scoured the neighborhood for days to find all the "pretties" people had brought with them from their other lives.

William and John sat down to one of the best meals they had ever eaten. Roast beef, pork, turkey and a lot of fowls were laid out on platters. Jean Baptiste, a nearby neighbor, had brought roasted quail and partridges.

"I still like venison best of all," William said to John.

"So do I, brother. Some things never change," John said, looking away into the woods.

Wild plums, crab apples stewed in maple sugar, corn, beans, persimmon pudding, all were delicious, but the best thing was the bread made from wheat someone had brought from "over yonder in the Whitewater country," from John Conner's town. And Lavina, John's wife, had made the wedding cake from her famous pound cake recipe.

A few months later, Elizabeth and William were enjoying a rare walk along White River. The June sun and the brightness of the yellow violets on the path almost made Elizabeth forget about the work that was waiting for her at home in the cabin. She pulled loose the ribbons on her bonnet and looked downstream.

"Look, William. Here comes the keelboat! Isn't it exciting they are stopping here now?"

"Yes," William said. "It's pickin' up what's left over of last year's grain crop and some pickled pork. There's so much produce, this is the best way to get it to the city. Lucky there's high water this spring. White River is pretty rocky and shallow. The boats can't always navigate it."

It was hard to get crops to market. There weren't many roads, because the woods were all around. The few roads there were, were so bad horses sometimes sank up to their knees in mud. A wagon loaded down with tons of grain had a hard time getting through. Perhaps keelboats could help haul the grain from the Horseshoe Prairie area.

Elizabeth had watched a few keelboats pass Conner's Prairie, as they were now calling William's land, before. The boats were fifty feet long and about ten feet wide. They had a roof over the top, except for a narrow deck which ran all the way around the boat. The deck was very important. On it the pole men stood, with long wooden poles which they stuck in the water.

"That doesn't look like very hard work, William," Elizabeth said to her husband as they watched the boat go by.

"That's because the boat is just floatin' downstream now. They're just being sure there are no snags. But it's lots harder when they come back up. The current fights them, so they say. The steerin' man tells them to set those poles up the stream, and they do. Then they have to strain and push the boat as they walk along the deck."

"Don't they ever pull the boat with a rope?"

"If there's a path along the shore they can do that. We don't have a good one here."

"Look," she cried, as they watched the keelboat disappearing around the bend. "There are people on it, riding to the new capital, Indianapolis. That boat's a combination log cabin, barnyard and general store all rolled into one!"

William chuckled to see the kegs, boxes, pigs, fowls, dogs, dishes, and people all floating around the bend of his White River, which used to be so quiet and wild.

"Well, I'm glad to see them," said Elizabeth. It means we're turning into a real settlement. More people are coming in every week."

It was true. One of them, to William's great joy, was John Conner, his brother. John Conner, who always liked to grab opportunities, had grabbed a new one. The lands from the Treaty of St. Mary's were being sold by the government. John himself bought the land at Horseshoe Prairie. His brother's land was not part of the parcel John bought. In fact, William was still trying to get the government to sell him the land where his house stood.

The Finches and other people had to move a short distance away when John bought Horseshoe Prairie. They had been "squatters," anyway. If a pioneer built a cabin and planted a few rows of corn on unsold land, he could usually

93

buy the land when it came up for sale. That is, if someone didn't buy it all first. That is what John Conner did. He had the money to afford the whole piece of land, so he bought it.

The settlers weren't too sure they liked it. "John Conner had the longest pole and got the persimmon," they said to each other.

But they liked what he did for them all. By 1823 John Conner had built a sawmill, grist mill, and a carding machine for wool.

The sawmill cut good boards for settlers' homes. The gristmill ground their corn and wheat. The carding machine pulled out the kinks and dirt in wool and made it ready for spinning. The settlers were glad for John after all!

"Sometimes I wish you would move a little faster, William," Elizabeth said as she rocked her new baby in the rocking chair a few months later. The baby was named Lavina, after John's wife. "John is putting up all kinds of big things at Horseshoe Prairie so near us. I think it's time for us to make plans. This house just doesn't suit our needs any more." She wrapped another blanket around little Lavina. The cabin was drafty.

"Well, I agree with you. The new capital is growin' so fast and it's not too far from us. I've been thinkin' for a long while about buildin' a house here. I have the money, from m' tradin' days." He thought of the silver left in the trunk. "And the farm is doin' well."

They picked out a pretty site south of the cabin and William Conner started his brick house in 1823. "Since I have a new life, I'm sure to need a new house to go with it," he said.

It was a beautiful home, built with solid, thick bricks. The woodwork was yellow poplar wood.

John helped William employ skilled craftsmen to make the fine mantels, stairways and glass-door cupboards. There was a center hall and two big rooms, on both the first and second floors. Each room had a wide fireplace, and the kitchen had a loft where a cook could sleep.

"We may even have hired help," William thought. "I wonder what Running Wolf would think of his old blood brothers now?"

Even though he was sometimes surprised himself at all the fancy things in the new house, William was really very proud. Visitors came often now, and they said complimentary things about the home.

It was a delight to see this two-story, impressive house out in the middle of a forest. Small cabins were the rule in the woods. Just as people had always looked for William Conner's trading post, now they looked for his home.

This fine house became the center of everything. The circuit court and the county commissioners of the newly founded Hamilton County met there.

Many important people came, too. One of them was Charles C. Trowbridge, a man who was writing a book about the Delaware Indians. Governor Cass of Michigan had hired Trowbridge to go around and find out all he could about them. The U.S. Government wanted a report on them.

Trowbridge spent three months living at William's house talking with him, and with Captain Pipe, the Delaware Chief who was still in the area.

Trowbridge had a notebook, and he often asked William to help him understand the Delaware customs. "I have heard of the 'Sweating Rite' ceremony, William," he said one day. "But I don't quite understand it. It has something to do with the number twelve. Can you help me?"

"I think so. My old friend Running Wolf, a strong and brave Delaware man, invited me to the 'sweatin' rite' once when I was up with Chief Anderson.

"The number twelve is important to it. Running Wolf hunted and killed two powerful bears for this ceremony. He chose ten other men besides me to attend.

95

"The purpose of the ceremony was to make sure a person is right with the Great Spirit. We ate bear meat and we went into the 'oven' to sacrifice to Him.

"Running Wolf, as I recollect, built an oven of twelve different pieces of wood, each one from a different kind of tree. Twelve, not more, not less. Then he covered up the pieces of wood tightly with blankets to make a little tent.

"Running Wolf heated twelve medium sized stones as hot as they could get and put them into the oven. All twelve us who were part of the ceremony crawled inside. We watched Running Wolf sprinkle tobacco over the stones. This was his offerin' of prayer to the Great Spirit.

"He gave me twelve measures of wampum. 'Go out of the oven and pray loudly to The Great Spirit facing the rising sun, then return,' he told me.

"This done," said William, "I crawled back inside the oven, ate some of the bear meat and stayed, roastin' so to speak, 'till I passed out from the heat. The ceremony wouldn't work unless I stayed till I had to be dragged out."

Trowbridge was scribbling in his notebook. He was sitting at one of William's fancy new desks.

"Would the Indians go in and out of the oven twelve times?" he asked William.

"To be sure they were right with the Great Spirit they were 'sposed to do it twelve times. But I could never stand it more than twice," William told him.

Trowbridge learned many important things about the Delawares while he was visiting William Conner. His findings were written in the Cass-Trowbridge report for the government.

Another visitor in the 1820's to the fine new house was Josiah F. Polk. He knew that John, and now William, were very smart when it came to buying and selling land, land speculation, as it is called. William loved his land and knew other people would always want land too. If he had plenty, it would always be a kind of savings account. Something he

96

could use for his future, a kind of "playing card held back," as he had said before.

By January, 1823, the Legislature in Indianapolis had set up Hamilton County. When counties were set up, it was common for men of those times to buy up land and lay out their own towns. "Town builders" they called these men. William and Mr. Polk bought one hundred acres on the east bank of White River, hoping they could become town builders.

"We'll do it right," William said. "Donate land for a courthouse and a jail, maybe even for a seminary (high school).

The Hamilton County commissioners accepted their plan and soon William was selling off lots in his new town. It was to be called Noblesville.

As for John, opportunity was still his middle name. John Conner had big plans for Horseshoe Prairie. But he also had some plans up the river about thirteen miles. He saw opportunity in the new town of Indianapolis.

Chapter Nine
Early Indianapolis

Indianapolis in the 1820's was a small, country town. The forest was still king in the new capital of Indiana, and it spread its canopy from one end of Washington Street to the other. Huge sugar, walnut, ash, honey locust, and elms almost swallowed up the log buildings that were the town.

Smart businessman that he was, John headed for this new center of activity. There were only a few stores in 1823 in

Indianapolis. Surely they could use a fine new establishment run by an old hand in the mercantile business. John looked for a partner and found Richard Tyner. Together they founded Conner, Tyner and Company.

Washington Street was still a bumpy, uneven trail. There was talk that after a while it would be cleared so it could become part of the National Road, and pioneers would use it to cross from Ohio to Illinois. It wasn't much, now, though. John had to pick his way around stumps and thick brush on his way to his store one afternoon in the fall of 1824. He had been busy running for assemblyman, and he had not had time to check up on his store for a few days. His partner Richard actually ran the store, but that didn't mean John didn't have a say in its operation.

"Thank God we haven't had rain lately," he thought, looking down at the crusty mud beneath his feet. "This road gets as nasty as a pig wallow."

He watched a train of horses loaded with baggage make its way down the risky path in front of him, jolting along to keep out of the way of the stumps and deep mud holes. Dogs and chickens roamed in nearby gardens, picking around among bread crusts and other garbage people threw out on the street.

"I'm glad it's still daylight," John thought as he neared his store. "I'll have to ask the assembly about getting some street lights. We can't have people stumbling into tree stumps and even robbers sometimes at night. Maybe we can vote on it at the next session." His boots squished through fresh, black mud.

"Too bad the commissioners chose a place that was down in the swamps," John thought. People got sick in the swamp areas, with agues, but also with typhoid fever and cholera, awful diseases that killed many people. "There's a lot of sickness here. Still, we do have a good water supply. That's important."

He took a long, cool drink from a roadside well. Indianapolis was located on a sandy bed of good water which was only twelve feet down.

John glanced around the town and compared it in his mind with some other cities he'd been to in the past. Travelling as an Indian interpreter and on business for his old store at Connersville, he'd seen Washington, D.C. and Cincinnati and Philadelphia. He knew Indianapolis had a long way to go.

Still, stores were popping up everywhere in this new village: tailors, shoemakers, clock repair men, cabinet makers. Even "Fancy Tom's" barber shop had opened. There were doctors' and lawyers' offices. John saw with an approving eye that the new courthouse was coming along nicely, with a bell tower being built that would rise 100 feet in the air. That would help the city look less like a wilderness.

Roads were always the worst problem, in the city of Indianapolis and in the state itself. Until Indiana could solve the road problem, it would not grow as it should. The farmers needed to get their produce in to town. They couldn't always use the rivers like John and William and the folks at Horseshoe Prairie did. After all, not all towns were on the rivers. Even at Horseshoe Prairie, the river wasn't deep enough for boats at all seasons of the year.

"These roads are mostly old Indian trails," John thought. "Armies crossing the state, or even pioneers coming in, have no good way to go." It was true.

One man on horseback followed in the trail of another. The trail was all right until they reached a low or swampy place. Then you couldn't see the trail and had to guess. If mud was too bad, someone put logs crosswise over the trail. This was called a "corduroy road," but it didn't help much.

"We've got to do something," John told himself. Perhaps the assembly, when it met in the new courthouse, would begin talking about a road to Ft. Wayne, and one straight north to Michigan.

Now, walking over these bad roads, John had reached Conner and Tyner Store. He went in and nodded at his clerk, Alfred Harrison, a young man from his old neighborhood, the Whitewater region. "Good afternoon, Alfred," he said. "How's business?" Business, of course, was always first in the mind of John Conner.

"Fine, sir, but we seem to have had a run on umbrellas. Looks like folk are gettin' ready for the fall rains."

John nodded and went to check the wooden shelves for himself. There was plenty of stock on the shelves, rows of cotton, silk, wool, linen. He had a section of combs, brushes, parasols, shawls, but sure enough, no umbrellas left.

"I'm surprised Mr. Tyner has let the stock go down. I see the new style bonnets are also out of stock. I'll make a note of it, Harrison, when we place the next order for Cincinnati."

John made his way past more rows of hardware, of saddles, spelling books and spices. He was looking for his partner, Richard Tyner.

"There you are, you old devil!" John exclaimed. His partner Richard was sleeping next to the whisky barrel.

He would have to speak to Richard about minding the store better. He could do that later, though. Now it was time for supper. "How's about joining me for an early supper over at Widow Nowland's boarding house?" John asked, helping his partner up.

"Naw—let's go to Major Carter's Tavern, down by the courthouse. More action there."

John nodded. He would have liked Widow Nowland's, but Carter's was almost as good. He spoke to Harrison one last time about the stock and they left the store and headed towards supper.

"My wife's got a good bunch of pies, hot from the oven," the innkeeper said as they settled themselves at a round, maple table. He put down two pewter mugs and a jug of applejack to start them off.

"How about some venison?" John asked the innkeeper.

"No wild game tonight," the man answered. "Getting harder to scare any up, what with the town growing up so much."

John was disappointed. He still liked the wild game he had enjoyed in his youth. "I'll have the pork and potatoes, plenty of hot bread, too," he said to the innkeeper.

"Same for me," Richard said, drinking off his cider and pouring another. "I got some news for you about some of your Indian friends." Richard Tyner spoke in a slightly mocking voice. He did not like Indians.

"Tell me what you know," John said. He settled into a ladder-back chair and silently drank his applejack. His eyes roved about the room. This tavern was not bad, as taverns went. It had a large sitting room, a dining room with a bar, and a separate kitchen wing. Still, it was not as nice as Wid-

102

ow Nowland's. There were too many people drinking too much, and fights, of a Saturday night. Sometimes Richard was one of the men who fought.

Richard poured from the jug and began to talk about the Indians. "I'm talkin' about those Shawnees and Miamis that had trouble at their camp up in Madison County? With three women and four little ones with 'em?"

"It was an outrage!" John said angrily. "Those Indians were fine traders, with many furs, and the white traders grew jealous." The Delawares might be leaving, but the Miamis and Potawatomis and a few Shawnees were still in the state. They were having real troubles.

A man named Harper, a trader from Missouri Territory, got wind of all the furs the Indian camp had. He and some of the settlers tricked the Indians, took their furs and killed them.

John continued to be angry at being reminded of the massacre. "Trick a harmless family of Indians, kill 'em like a herd of deer—that's awful!"

"I s'pose so. You would think so, I guess. But you're an Indian lover," Richard Tyner mumbled.

"Indians are men too, though the settlers around here don't seem to think so. They like a good meal, love their wives, play with their little ones. I should know."

"Well, I suppose it ain't right to kill anybody, even a Indian," Richard said. "What I was going to tell you is that they are goin' to punish Harper and his friends. Hang 'em, so they say. So the Indians' spirits can rest in peace, I guess." Then he was silent. He was not a bad man, just like most of the settlers in Indiana. His fear of Indians went back to the days of the old Indian wars. He didn't like "the savages," as the settlers called them.

The innkeeper brought them more applejack and John drank it in silence, brooding. Would troubles with his old friends the Indians never stop? Probably not until all the

103

Indians were removed from Indiana. It seemed like the white settlers and Indians could not live together.

"It's bad for us all when these things happen. What if we had a bloody Indian uprising over those murders?" John asked. He was not only worried about the Indians; he was afraid that his new group at Horseshoe Prairie would be in danger.

The innkeeper set two steaming plates of food down and bustled away. John was not hungry any more.

Richard had certainly not lost his appetite. He gulped his food. He chewed and snorted like a hungry hog. John watched him. He had never been much for manners, but some of the folk in this new town—well, the Indians would have thought them rude.

"I guess it's good they're hangin' Harper and his crew, John," Richard said finally. "Nobody wants to get the Miami and Shawnee riled up. But as long as the Indians are in Indiana, there will be trouble."

There were lots of times where Indians and white people clashed lately. The Indians had reserved lands, "reservations," but white people built cabins right on the edges of the Indians' lands. If the settlers had their way, soon their would not be an Indian left in Indiana. They wanted them gone! John's old friend from the Assembly, John Tipton, was an Indian agent and wanted treaties for more land to be opened up for settlers. That meant the Miamis and Potawatomis would have to give up the lands they still held.

John pushed back his untouched dinner plate and called the innkeeper to pay the bill for supper. "Tyner—see that you mind the stock at the store better. Remember the old saying, 'Keep your store and your store will keep you.' I expect you to do just that." Then John strode out into the brisk, fall night air that he had always enjoyed. But as the cool air from off White River rushed at him, his spirits sank. His heart was not at peace.

Soon he was called on to interpret again. In 1826 John Tipton decided to take LeGros, a Miami chief, to Washington to talk about a new treaty to get more land. Tipton asked John Conner to go with him. John agreed, thinking he might be able to be of some help, and at least interpret the Indian's words rightly.

The trip went well until they reached Maryland. On the trail just outside the town of Hagerstown, John began to feel ill. "Why do I have to get a fever now?" he thought.

Beads of perspiration began to form on his forehead, even though it was cold outside. It was the dead of winter.

"Let's find an inn, so I can rest," he told Tipton.

"We've got one room left," a large woman who ran the inn they settled in said. "One of you will have to sleep on the floor." Her eyes coldly scanned Chief LeGros of the Miamis.

LeGros pulled his heavy robe about him and stood taller. He had learned not to let insults from white people bother him. He went down the hall and John followed after him.

John was bothered by the woman's rude ways. It was the same old thing that had been troubling him lately. It wasn't just that the white men wanted the Indians land, or were afraid of them. There was more. Now that the Indians were no longer something to be afraid of, now that they were giving up their land in treaties, people didn't respect them. They treated Indians like hogs or dogs. If they saw Indian children in a village, they did not speak. If a white man stole something from an Indian or even killed a tribesman, state law did not often punish the white man.

This woman innkeeper was like most Americans—she thought of Indians as "barbaric," almost like animals. "Well, I can't worry about this all the time, I guess," John Conner thought finally. "I have business to take care of."

The woman had brought them down the musty, narrow hall to a room. There was a ragged curtain in the middle to divide it. "Men on this side of the curtain, women on 't other," she said, leading them inside.

"The tin wash basin is for women only, so hands off it. You can use the horse trough outside. I'll take the Indian to the stable. If we get full, we may need the bedroom floor. I have to save it for white men."

"I need to lie down, right now," John thought, feeling hot and sick. He had stopped looking at the woman, and when he heard the door slam, he knew she and LeGros had gone.

John sat down on the bed. He felt the hard boards through the straw mattress. "I've slept better in the woods," he thought. At least there were no bed bugs to bite him. He pulled up a dirty blanket and went to sleep.

He woke aching from head to toe. "You can't travel on horseback any longer, John. I'm hiring a hack," John Tipton told his friend. He went out to call a horse-drawn, covered cart.

They came to Washington City, as it was called then. John was feeling worse. He bedded down in the Indian Queen Hotel. Tipton decided to take LeGros for new clothes and give John time to rest.

Snow whipped in icy curls outside the small glass window of the hotel. John fell into fitful sleep. He dreamed he was in a canoe, as he was when he was a child. He saw a large white figure floating above the canoe. "What do you want from me?" he cried out.

The figure grew larger. It had sleek white feathers and sharp, bright eyes. It was a white owl.

"Are you happy with your choices, my friend?"

"Choices?" John asked, afraid of the owl.

"You chose white over Indian. Are you content now?" It beat its wings against the canoe. John thrashed his arms about trying to beat back the owl, and woke up on the cold floor.

"I chose white. I guess I thought it was the only choice I had," he said, weakly, to nobody in particular.

106

John did not feel much better the next few days, but he had to go with Tipton and LeGros to the War Department. There the government men talked about the new treaty. They discussed the lands near the Wabash. LeGros shrugged his shoulders. There was nothing much Indians could do, he knew, when white men wanted land.

John was more than ready to head home. It was hard to pretend he was feeling all right when he felt awful.

The stage coach horn blew as it arrived in Washington to pick up LeGros, John Conner, and John Tipton.

The stage had been placed on sled runners because of the snow. John sank into large buffalo robes and put a foot-warmer under his feet. They all whizzed along on the slick snow until they reached the bottom of an impossibly steep hill.

"All first class passengers get out and walk," the driver called. "All second class passengers get out and push."

John was glad he was riding first class. He barely had enough energy to walk up the hill, let alone push a coach up!

His head swam and he stumbled and fell in the snow. Running Wolf's words seem to float in his mind. "You are weak, John Conner. The Delawares do not act weak. You must be a strong Indian man."

"I'm not weak," John Conner said aloud. "And I'm not an Indian. I thought I told you that before."

Tipton and LeGros gave him odd looks. Then they helped him up the hill.

When John Conner returned to Indianapolis, he was still in poor health. The fever seemed to hang on, and he felt weak and dizzy most of the time. Still, he did not let that stop him. Years of wilderness living had hardened his soul and body. He continued running his store. He served as Indian interpreter at the some of the treaties where the Miami Indians signed away their lands in northern Indiana.

But he had never really recovered from the strains of the trip to Washington in the bitterly cold weather. Finally he was forced to take to his bed. The family called his brother, William, to come up from Conner Prairie. John lay at his hotel, the Washington Hall.

A strong wind, promising rain, ripped at the curtains of the bedroom. Lavina held back the curtains. The moon came out from behind a black cloud, sending moonbeams into the room.

William remembered other moonlit April evenings when he and his brother had walked the trails to hunt, using the moon to light their way.

"Lying there, so still, he does not look like the rich white merchant that he is," William thought. "His skin is so dark and wrinkled by the sun, his hair so lank. No wonder they say he, and I too, have never stopped looking and talking like Indians."

"Will, take care of my sons," John whispered from the bed. "And my businesses, see to them."

It was like John, William thought, to think about his business in his dying breath. And why not? He had worked hard for what he had. William leaned close to his brother. What was it he was saying? *"Xu lapi knewel."* "Goodby" in Delaware.

There were three ways to say "goodbye" in Delaware and John had chosen "I will see you again," William thought. His mother's—and the Moravian's—Christian training was still with him. *"Xu lapi knewel.* Goodbye, till we meet again, brother to you," William whispered in his brother's ear. And then John Conner was gone.

The William Conner House, built in 1823

Chapter Ten

The New Town of Noblesville

"I will carry on for you, John," William thought as he walked down Washington Street in Indianapolis, that spring of 1826, trying to fight back the sadness he felt. "You worked so hard to build everything up. I will see our Conner name lives on."

And live on it did. William continued to increase his land holdings in Hamilton County and operated John's mills. By now, he owned more than 4,000 acres in Hamilton County. Elizabeth and William's family continued to grow, while John's sons prospered under their uncle's care.

John's store in Indianapolis was kept open until 1833, though it was located in different spots as time passed.

One glorious fall day in 1837 William Conner strolled through the town of Noblesville. He had finally left his Conner's Prairie farm to move into town. It was easier and better for his family now to live in the village. What a sense of pride he felt now, living in the town he had helped found.

He had left his prairie home with one worry still not solved. He did not yet have the legal title to his farm, a title he had tried to get for so long. Governor Jonathan Jennings had promised the land would be William's, during the time of the Treaty of St. Mary's. William had lived on the land with his Indian wife, and that made him entitled to it. But it was taking so long! It had been seventeen years since Mekinges left and he wanted a clear title to the farm.

Still, here he was in Noblesville now. Someone else was farming the land out on the prairie for William. Now he had a store in town, a general store. He had a partner, too, a man named John J. Will. William decided he would go see his partner. He had told him to order a painted sign for their general store, even though Mr. Will was very busy now at the new cobbler shop he had just opened. He ran the general store in the mornings, and made shoes at the cobbler shop in the afternoons. There was lots of business activity in Noblesville these days.

As William walked in, John Will was at his cobbler's bench, talking to a customer. "I don't know, George," John was saying. "I still think it was them wildcats that snatched your lambs. Not the bald eagles."

112

The farmer spoke a few more words and left, shaking his head. Trying to make all of this area into good farms had its problems. Squirrels scrambled over the plowed fields by the thousands after woods were cut down and ate up corn. You couldn't get rid of them. Sometimes locusts, a kind of grasshopper-like insect, came and stripped all the fields bare and even ate all the oak leaves off the trees. Floods came up when White River got high. And now, wild animals were carrying off stock.

Still, it was good site. The village of Noblesville was right in the middle of some of the best land in the state. The village was growing like a cornfield in June, and all these new shops, like the general store, and Mr. Will's cobbler's shop, proved it!

Mr. Will had a lap board he was using to stretch a shoe. "I have to run around like a hen with its head chopped off to work at these two places now," he said. "But I did the job you told me to. I ordered the sign for our store. The schoolteacher's been making it. Red and blue, 'twill be."

"You seem to have lots of customers already," William told him. "It confounds me that you have enough energy to have two businesses! I have enough trouble just keepin' our store goin'." He was feeling older these days.

"Yes. But Noblesville needed a cobbler shop, and with the money we have been making in the store, I invested in a new venture! Opportunity! That's what America is about, isn't it?"

William nodded. That's certainly what his brother John had thought.

"Want to see what I have here, William?" John Will asked, pointing to the table. "It's one of the new editions of the Noblesville paper."

"I haven't seen today's issue. Let me take a look," William said with interest. Every town needed a newspaper, and now his village had one. People read the newspaper out loud to their families every night by the light of oil lamps. The

113

Noblesville newspaper had stories of wild animals and famous men, doings of the United States government, and news of wars in other countries. It was interesting entertainment.

"I want to show you an advertisement for my new cobbler shop," John Will told William. There was a box on the back page, with a high-topped shoe in it. A fancy border around the edge was supposed to make everyone look at the ad. "Shoes, made ready to wear. Best morocco pumps for church and Spanish riding boots for town wear," it said.

The new newspaper looked fine and professional. "A newspaper and a cobbler shop. Real signs of an up-to-date town," William thought. As he put down the paper, he remembered the moccasins he and Mekinges used to wear out and mend on the trail. He had not heard from her, and he did not see his children as much as he had hoped. Time and many miles had put a distance between them which was not easy to bridge.

William stood up to watch John Will work on the wooden pegs used to hold shoes together. Everything was still handmade, with care, here in this little shop. A stick of sugar maple was taken from the woodpile and sawed into blocks. These blocks were then cut into pegs of the desired lengths after they had dried by the fire.

It was the same in all the little shops along the street—everything crafted by hand, with most of the raw materials coming right from the forest which was not far from the town's edge. The round wooden heads for hats to sit on in the hat shop had to be made by hand, from white pine, with a drawknife. The benches in the schoolroom were made of oak in the carpenter's shop. So was the schoolmaster's desk. Even baskets and containers were made of woven ashwood bark and fibers. Wood was one thing there was plenty of.

The men of Noblesville had made the beds, the chests of drawers, and even the tables and chairs for many of their own homes.

114

William Conner, oil portrait in the Conner House by Jacob Cox, from an ambrotype now in possession of Conner Prairie.

William told John Will that he liked the new advertisement, and the store, too. "I'll go pick up our store sign at the schoolhouse," he said.

He stepped out onto the corner. There was a street sign with his name on it to mark the corner—"Conner Street." William looked at it. "This place has come a long way since Polk and I laid it out," William thought.

He walked down the street towards the one-room log school. William's old friends from Horseshoe Prairie, Joseph Willison and Israel Finch, were clanging away on the anvil of the blacksmith's shop, as he passed. He looked up to see a tavern sign swinging in the wind. George Shirts, another friend, drew a lot of folk to this "ordinary" on Eighth Street.

William came to the edge of the muddy "School" street, then crossed on boards to the other side. From out the door of the schoolhouse floated the sounds of children's singing and suddenly, with a pang of tenderness, he thought of the

115

Moravian schoolhouse where he and John had spent happy hours so long ago.

"Hail Columbia, happy land," the Noblesville children sang. And Columbia, America, was a happy land, William thought. At least for the people in Indiana. Most of them, anyway. The Potawatomi, some of the last of the Indians in Indiana, were getting ready to go west to Kansas. The government had decided they could not stay, not even on the last reservation that had been given to them. They would have to march west. They were not happy in "Columbia, happy land."

William put his head in at the door and the schoolmaster, a well-fed man with a bald head, smiled and came over to greet him.

"I have the sign right here," he said. "Children, practice the verse of the continents," he said as he went to get the sign from inside his desk.

As William left, he smiled again with pride. The schoolhouse had more children every year. One student, the oldest boy in the school, was even planning to go over to the new Wabash academy at Crawfordsville.

There was no doubt but that the town was getting to be an important one. "After all, it is the county seat," William told himself.

"I'm not going to get too fancy in my store, though," William thought. "Not going to stock satin ball gowns, like John did in Indianapolis. It's not my way." He told himself he had better hurry home. There was a play-party tonight, and his family would be "rarin' to go"—out to a harvest festival and corn shucking at Conner's Prairie.

As the wagon rounded a bend in the road, through stubble cornfields made golden by the setting sun, they came to the place William had known for so long. Seeing the old fields and woods made him remember for a moment his old life. It had been difficult having to change so much, but it had to be done. Still, sometimes he missed his Indian family.

116

"Here we are," his fourteen-year-old daughter Lavina cried. She jumped down and twirled away, rosy-cheeked and happy. She was looking shyly at a boy from a nearby farm. Sides were already being chosen for the corn husking. William's farm manager was having the party.

Corn had been heaped in a long pile in the middle of the barn. Although husking the corn was work, most people liked to make a game of it. They got together and raced to see who could shuck the most corn out of the pile.

Someone put up a wooden rail dividing the corn pile, and the contest was on. Off went the husks, rip, jerk, toss. Hands flew, ears of corn thumped on the dirt barn floor. Everyone cheered in excitement. The unhusked pile grew lower, and by nine o'clock the floor was clean. Lavina's side had finished first.

Supper was set on tables out under the trees. William could hear Lavina singing,

Green grow the rushes, Oh!
Kiss her quick and let her go!
But don't you muss her ruffle, Oh.

The sound of the fiddle began and people began stamping and clapping to the "Virginia Reel." The barn dance had begun. There were so many fancy dances these days.

He seemed to hear in his mind the words of an Indian song, one of his favorites. *"Yoh an awa gow haw."* It was that simple. As simple as Indian life itself.

William walked to the ridge overlooking his property. Corn stood in shocks in the fields that sloped gently away to White River, as far as the eye could see, and an early evening river mist was rising to envelop the prairie. Birds were swooping and gathering on the horizon to begin their flight south, as they had since he was a child among the Indians, as they always would in this land of farms and woods and rivers. Soon plentiful fields of wheat would be planted for spring harvesting.

"If only John could be here to share this with me," William thought. But it was not a sad thought. William was content with himself, and he thought John would be glad to see what he had done with their lands.

He had come a long way in his life—they both had. From an exciting and mysterious beginning with Indians, to a place among the best-known men in the Old Northwest. He gazed out at White River, calm and clear. He could still imagine his Delaware friends kneeling on its banks, preparing to put in fishing lines. To them it was a sacred place, a place spirits blessed. Now white boys and girls chased each other about and dogs nipped at their heels. Somehow, he felt even now the presence of the tribal peoples, understanding the woodlands, caring for all living things, as Running Wolf had. Their spirit would live on in Indiana.

"Yes," William thought, "life does go on. Running Wolf and Mekinges taught me that. We all have choices to make, and I can live with mine." He turned to join the crowd at the barn, content with himself.

His past, far-away and exciting life with the Delawares would always hold a special place in his heart. William knew no other white man in Indiana could boast this unusual relationship with the Indians. William, though, would never boast.

Like his brother he was quietly strong, honest and ready to respond to opportunities and the future. John and William Conner were wise brothers of the forest, and their legend lives on.

CONNER PRAIRIE TODAY: FUN FOR THE ENTIRE FAMILY

History comes alive for children, teens and adults at Conner Prairie, a living history museum six miles northeast of Indianapolis. Three special areas cover 55 acres of the museum's property, bringing three different kinds of historic interpretation to 20th century visitors.

First, there's the cornerstone of Conner Prairie, the 1823 William Conner home. This federal-style house features interpreters who are knowledgeable about the lives and times of Indiana frontiersman, fur trader and statesman William Conner. Visitors see where Conner and his family lived from 1823 to 1837 and learn how he settled central Indiana and was instrumental in the development of the state. Nearby, there's a loom house where skilled textile workers demonstrate spinning and the weaving of intricate blankets, coverlets and linens.

Second, there's the 1836 Village of Prairietown, where costumed interpreters bring history to life by role-playing "residents" of the small community. Here, it is *always* 1836 Indiana, and these specially trained men and women make you believe you have entered another time. Chat with Mrs. Zimmerman, who keeps the Golden Eagle Inn, and sit a spell on the front porch of the Whitaker's Store, people watching. Take a lesson at the school and watch the blacksmith working at the forge. There are 29 buildings total, from Dr. Campbell's spacious home in the center of town to the pottery complex.

Finally, after you've learned about Indiana history through the eyes of William Conner and talked with people who might have lived in 1836, try the chores, pastimes and crafts of these early settlers at the Pioneer Adventure Area. This hands-on log cabin area features games, spinning and weaving, candle dipping, woodworking and seasonal activities—and visitors are encouraged to try them all.

Live history through Conner Prairie's three historic areas and by touring the new modern museum center, which features an orientation presentation on early Indiana and the development of Conner Prairie, changing exhibits gallery, and a bakery and restaurant, both of which serve some historic style foods.

The museum center is open year-around, and the historic areas are open for regular touring April through November. December features evening Conner Prairie by Candlelight tours, and January through March are Hearthside Suppers in the William Conner home.

For more information, call (317) 776-6000 or write to Conner Prairie. 13400 Allisonville Road, Noblesville, IN 46060.

The 1836 Village at Conner Prairie features costumed interpreters who role-play "residents" of the small community. Featured are 29 buildings, including a store, blacksmith's shop, pottery, doctor's home and inn.

Miss Emma Osborn, school mistress, walks down River Road to visit with Mrs. Whitaker.

Mrs. George Washington Campbell (Harriet) wife of the village doctor and founder, works on fancy sewing in her home in Prairietown.

Mr. Whitaker, the storekeeper in Conner Prairie's 1836 Village of Prairietown, looks over his ledger. Costumed interpreters role-play 19th century "residents" of the small village.

The Pioneer Adventure Area at Conner Prairie features hands-on learning, where children and adults can try the crafts, chores and pastimes of early settlers.

SOME DELAWARE WORDS
From The Cass Trowbridge Manuscript

Arrow	Nape
Ball	Tock-au-sin
Bear	Muhk ¿
Bow	Maw-taut
Boy	Pe-lo-wi-chitch
Bad	Ma-tit
Buffalo	Sa-sa-le-a
Cat	Po-cheeze
Canoe	Uh-muk-ko
Corn	Quos-quim
Dog	Maw-kuh-na-o
Deer	Au-tooh
Father	Nohe
Friend	Jose
Fire	Tin-da-o
Girl	Uck-qua-sis
Good	Wylet
House	Wa-quaw
Mother	Guek
Owl	Ko-ko
Pigeon	Ma-ma
Raccoon	Es-pun
Rock	Au-sin
Saddle	Aw-puh-pone
Tree	Ma-took
Water	Ba

Acknowledgments

Advisers for this book were:

J. Martin West, Director of Ft. Ligonier in Western Pennsylvania

David G. Vanderstel, Ph.D. Senior Historian Conner Prairie

Julie Hines, Volunteer Coordinator, Schoenbrunn Village State Memorial, New Philadelphia, Ohio

Thomas Krasean, Indiana Historical Society

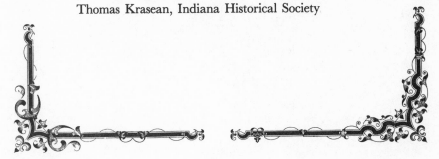